DATE DUE

FRANZ
KAFKA

COMPREHENSIVE RESEARCH
AND STUDY GUIDE

BLOOM'S
MAJOR
NOVELISTS

EDITED AND WITH AN
INTRODUCTION BY HAROLD BLOOM

CURRENTLY AVAILABLE

FRANZ
KAFKA

COMPREHENSIVE RESEARCH
AND STUDY GUIDE

BLOOM'S
MAJOR
NOVELISTS

EDITED AND WITH AN INTRODUCTION
BY HAROLD BLOOM

CHELSEA HOUSE
PUBLISHERS
A Haights Cross Communications Company
Philadelphia

Printed and bound in the United States of America.

First Printing
1 3 5 7 9 8 6 4 2

Library of Congress Cataloging-in-Publication Data
Franz Kafka / edited with introduction by Harold Bloom.
      p. cm. —(Bloom's major novelists)
Includes bibliographical references and index.
   ISBN 0-7910-7028-X
   1. Kafka, Franz, 1883–1924—Criticism and interpretation. I. Bloom,
Harold. II. Series.
   PT2621.A26 Z65 2002
   833'.912—dc21   2002013047

Chelsea House Publishers
1974 Sproul Road, Suite 400
Broomall, PA 19008-0914

http://www.chelseahouse.com

Contributing Editor: Aaron Tillman

Cover design by Terry Mallon

Layout by EJB Publishing Services

CONTENTS

USER'S GUIDE

This volume is designed to present biographical, critical, and bibliographical information on the author and the author's best-known or most important plays. Following Harold Bloom's editor's note and introduction is a concise biography of the author that discusses major life events and important literary accomplishments. A critical analysis of each play follows, tracing significant themes, patterns, and motifs in the work. An annotated list of characters supplies brief information on the main characters in each play.

A selection of critical extracts, derived from previously published material, follows each thematic analysis. In most cases, these extracts represent the best analysis available from a number of leading critics. Because these extracts are derived from previously published material, they will include the original notations and references when available. Each extract is cited, and readers are encouraged to use the original publications as they continue their research. A bibliography of the author's writings, a list of additional books and articles on the author and their work, and an index of themes and ideas conclude the volume.

As with any study guide, this volume is designed as a supplement to the works being discussed, and is in no way intended as a replacement for those works. The reader is advised to read the text prior to using this study guide, and to keep it accessible for quick reference.

ABOUT THE EDITOR

Harold Bloom is Sterling Professor of the Humanities at Yale University and Henry W. and Albert A. Berg Professor of English at the New York University Graduate School. He is the author of over 20 books, and the editor of more than 30 anthologies of literary criticism.

Professor Bloom's works include *Shelley's Mythmaking* (1959), *The Visionary Company* (1961), *Blake's Apocalypse* (1963), *Yeats* (1970), *A Map of Misreading* (1975), *Kabbalah and Criticism* (1975), *Agon: Toward a Theory of Revisionism* (1982), *The American Religion* (1992), *The Western Canon* (1994), and *Omens of Millennium: The Gnosis of Angels, Dreams, and Resurrection* (1996). *The Anxiety of Influence* (1973) sets forth Professor Bloom's provocative theory of the literary relationships between the great writers and their predecessors. His most recent books include *Shakespeare: The Invention of the Human*, a 1998 National Book Award finalist, *How to Read and Why* (2000), and *Stories and Poems for Extremely Intelligent Children of All Ages* (2001).

Professor Bloom earned his Ph.D. from Yale University in 1955 and has served on the Yale faculty since then. He is a 1985 MacArthur Foundation Award recipient and served as the Charles Eliot Norton Professor of Poetry at Harvard University in 1987–88. In 1999 he was awarded the prestigious American Academy of Arts and Letters Gold Medal for Criticism. Professor Bloom is the editor of several other Chelsea House series in literary criticism, including BLOOM'S MAJOR SHORT STORY WRITERS, BLOOM'S MAJOR NOVELISTS, BLOOM'S MAJOR DRAMATISTS, BLOOM'S MODERN CRITICAL INTERPRETATIONS, BLOOM'S MODERN CRITICAL VIEWS, and BLOOM'S BIOCRITIQUES.

EDITOR'S NOTE

My introduction is a brief overview of *Amerika*, *The Castle*, and *The Trial*, emphasizing that they are to be considered as something other than novels in any traditional sense.

Of the Critical Views on *Amerika*, I particularly commend Heinz Politzer on Karl Rossmann's innocence, and Ritchie Robertson on Kafka's vision of the city. The novelist E.L. Doctorow is of particular interest, since his reflections stimulate the issue of Kafka's influence upon him.

The enigmatic *Castle* has a remarkable roster of exegetes, starting with the great novelist Thomas Mann, and with Albert Camus, theorist of the Absurd. Of great interest also are Charles Bernheimer on allegory, and Irving Howe, who attempts the impossible task of setting *The Castle* in a social context.

On *The Trial*, Ronald Gray investigates the book's uncanny comedy, while Henry Sussman gives a conspectus of the conflicting interpretations of the book.

INTRODUCTION

Harold Bloom

What in Kafka is not paradox is parable. One could set up a scale for his achievement, in descending order: aphorisms, fragments, parables, stories, diaries, letters, novels. The three novels—*Amerika*, *The Trial*, *The Castle*—are problematic. They are extraordinary, but something other than novels. I have been meditating upon Kafka for more than half a century, but I seldom reflect upon the novels, even *The Castle*. Clearly, we read the novels *because* they are Kafka's, which is not why we read Joyce's *Ulysses*, Proust's *In Search of Lost Time*, or Faulkner's *As I Lay Dying* and *Light in August*. Kafka was an unique writer, but only secondarily a novelist.

Amerika is palpably a Dickensian novel, a grotesque version of aspects of *David Copperfield*. The turbulence of innocence and guilt in Karl Rossman suggests the characteristic Dickens protagonist, David or Pip (in *Great Expectations*) working his way out of innocence into experience. The Kafka difference is that guilt is never to be doubted, though Karl Rossman receives his author's indulgence, as a kind of innocence in the last ditch.

Joseph K., in *The Trial*, is pursued on every side: by the grotesque servants of the Law, by deformed and predatory women, and by the unavailable books that state the Law. There is no hope for Joseph K., partly because he cannot realize his own self: it is internally exiled. We read on in fascination, and yet we receive none of the ordinary gratifications of the novel. Neither we nor Joseph K. ever can discover of what he is accused, and the squalid execution finally inflicted upon him possesses neither aesthetic dignity nor any glimmer of transcendence or even of meaning. Irony, exiling all meaning, is the literary condition of *The Trial*: we are engrossed, and yet perpetually frustrated if we ask the question: why was all this *necessary*? It is as though Kafka possesses a Gnostic Kabbalah, but is unable or unwilling to even begin divulging it to us.

The Castle certainly is Kafka's most impressive shadow of a novel, yet also the most enigmatic. We never know whether K.

the Surveyor has received a call from the Castle or not, but we suspect more and more strongly that the Castle is ruled by a Gnostic Archon or malign demiurge, Klamm, and that all who enter its sphere are doomed. Yet pragmatically, doom-eager K. cannot get into the Castle, which he needs to pass beyond if he is to achieve a reality that transcends the Castle's squalid illusions. K. is a Gnostic quester caught in the *kenoma*, the cosmological emptiness. He needs to confront Klamm in order to evade Klamm's world, but the hierarchy of the Castle holds him off.

Kafka jested that there was plenty of hope for God, but not for us. There are no traces of God in *The Castle*, but then there is, there can be, no coherence of plot either. K. never can learn whether his summoning by the Castle was a delusion or not, and the book is a labyrinth without an exit. And yet it is Kafka's labyrinth: fascinating, inescapable, the monument to a purposiveness without purpose.

Franz Kafka

Franz Kafka was born in Prague on July 3, 1883, the first born and only son of Hermann Kafka and Julie, nee Lowy. Hermann made a comfortable living as a fancy-goods shopkeeper. Julie would later give birth to two more boys, but neither lived. However, Kafka had three younger sisters: Gabriele "Elli," Valerie "Valli," and Ottilie "Otta." All three of Kafka's sisters later perished in Hitler's concentration camps.

When Kafka was six, he entered German primary school. He especially enjoyed reading and writing, and devoted much time to those aspects of his studies. In 1893, Franz progressed to the Old City German Secondary School. When he turned 13, he had his Bar Mitzvah, described on the invitation as a "Confirmation." The following year, there were anti-Semetic riots in Prague, but Franz's father's dry goods store was spared.

In 1901, Kafka graduated from secondary school and entered German University in Prague. His passion for reading and writing intensified, as he turned toward the philosophical and scientific writings of Darwin, Spinoza, and Nietzsche. He began his studies in Chemistry, but soon switched to Law. While at German University he met Max Brod, who would become his closest confidant throughout his life.

Kafka enjoyed an active social life and loved the outdoors, regularly planning long trips for his vacations. He traveled to Zuckmantel, Silesia in 1905 where he had his first love affair. He received his law degree from German University in 1906 and worked for a year in a law office. He then took a position at the Prague branch of the private insurance company Assicurazioni Generali. Kafka wrote while he worked at the insurance company, and his first publication—eight prose pieces—appeared in the review *Hyperion* in 1908.

Kafka also began keeping a diary as he established his writing career. In 1909, he and Max Brod traveled to Italy where they saw airplanes for the first time. He later wrote an article "The Aeroplanes in Brescia," which appeared in the daily paper

Bohemia. Kafka worked on his first book in 1912—*Meditation*—which would be published the next year. He also wrote his most famous short works during this time period, "The Judgment" and "The Metamorphosis," and worked on the novel that would be posthumously published, *Amerika*. Kafka became engaged to Felice Bauer in 1914 after a tumultuous two-year relationship, but the engagement was quickly called off. He wrote his short story "In the Penal Colony" in 1914.

Even though Franz Kafka wrote "The Metamorphosis" in 1912, he did not publish the story until 1915. That same year he won a literary award—the Theodor Fontane Prize—which included a prize of 800 marks. As a quiet, unobtrusive man, he detested the fame and recognition the award brought to him. Kafka continued to write though, and in 1916 he wrote many of the stories that would come to be published in the collection entitled *A Country Doctor*. During this time period Franz once again became engaged to Felice Bauer, but he was diagnosed with tuberculosis in September 1917, and the engagement was soon broken for the second and final time.

Kafka had a few brief relationships with women but disliked the idea of romance and sexual relations. Nevertheless, he met and quickly became engaged to Julie Wohryzek, the daughter of a custodian at a synagogue, in 1919. Following his father's overwhelming disapproval of the engagement, Kafka wrote the widely anthologized "Letter to His Father." In 1920, his collection *A Country Doctor* was published and his engagement to Julie Wohryzek was broken off.

Kafka took a sick leave from his job at the insurance company as his health rapidly deteriorated. In 1921, he was admitted into a sanatorium at Matliary in the Tatra mountains, where he began working on his novel *The Castle*. After he left the sanatorium, he completed *The Castle* and also wrote two of his shorter works of fiction: "A Hunger Artist" and "Investigations of a Dog." Two years later he met Dora Diamant—the last woman he would be romantically involved with—in Muritz on the Baltic Sea. He soon moved to Berlin to live with Dora, where he wrote "The Burrow."

Kafka's health began to deteriorate further in 1924. He wrote his final short story, "Josephine the Singer and the Mouse Folk" while in Berlin; afterwards his friend Max Brod took him back to Prague. On April 19, he entered Dr. Hoffman's sanatorium at Kierling, near Vienna. Soon after, he made the final edits on his collection of stories *A Hunger Artist.* On June 3, 1924, Franz Kafka died at the age of forty. He was buried in the Jewish Cemetery in Prague-Straschnitz on June 11.

PLOT SUMMARY OF

Amerika

Amerika, the first of Kafka's three posthumously published novels, opens as Karl Rossmann, "a poor boy of sixteen," stands on the deck of an ocean liner as it pulls into the New York harbor. Karl's parents insisted that he travel to America after a servant girl who had seduced him became pregnant. As the passengers begin to disembark, Karl remembers that he forgot his umbrella and asks an acquaintance named Franz Butterbaum to watch his box of belongings while he retrieves his umbrella.

Karl goes downstairs where he discovers that the short cut he had taken the previous few days has been blocked off, forcing him to take a more circuitous route, and he eventually loses his way. As he searches around for his whereabouts, he knocks on a random door and is told to enter. The room is occupied by the ship's stoker who invites him to sit down. The stoker tells Karl about the Chief Engineer named Schubal who discriminates against the Germans on the ship, despite the fact that they are on a German ship. As a result, he's decided to leave his post. Following a brief conversation, the stoker jumps up from his seat, grabs Karl by the arm and leads him out of his room. They walk to another room and knock on the door. Inside, the Head Purser, the Captain and other officers are engaged in a meeting. The stoker tells an attendant that he wants to speak to the Head Purser but is denied. Upset by the attendant's rebuke, Karl forces his way forward and states the stoker's case to the Captain and the Head Purser, suggesting that the stoker be allowed to voice his complaints in greater detail. Though the Captain concedes, the stoker lays down his complaints in an awkward and unconvincing way.

At that point, Schubal, the Chief Engineer, comes to the door and demands the opportunity to defend himself against the stoker. The Captain and the attendants are quiet as Schubal explains that he has come with witnesses. Instead of reacting to his statement, the Captain defers to the man with the bamboo cane who is standing beside him. This man asks Karl to repeat his name. Karl repeats his name and is met by bewildered eyes as the man reveals that he is Karl's uncle, Senator Edward Jacob. The Senator tells the Captain and the rest of the room the story of how Karl was seduced by his maid and shipped to America to avoid any custody battles. Though Karl tries to divert the conversation back to the stoker, his uncle makes it clear that the stoker's case should be left up to the Captain. When it's clear that Karl and his uncle are going to leave, Karl offers some emotional words of goodbye to the stoker, and then he and his uncle are escorted out of the ship and onto a rowboat which takes them to shore.

Karl is taken back to his uncle's lavish home in New York where he is set up with a spacious room that has a sizable writing desk and a balcony. Karl soon gets a piano and starts daily lessons in English. Karl proves to be an eager student, and as he increases his fluency, his uncle introduces him to more people. The Senator eventually decides that Karl should learn how to ride horses and sets up daily riding lessons for him with a man named Mr. Mack.

One day, Karl's uncle invites Karl to join him and two of his friends, Mr. Green and Mr. Pollunder, for dinner. Though Karl is quiet throughout most of the meal, Mr. Pollunder eventually starts asking questions about his journey. He becomes so impressed by Karl's answers that he invites him to his country house to meet his daughter. Karl's uncle gives his consent for the visit but refrains from stating a specific date and time. The following day, Karl's is summoned to one of his uncle's offices where Mr. Pollunder is waiting to take him to the country. Karl's uncle seems reluctant to let his nephew go, but his friend is persistent and eventually Karl and Mr. Pollunder leave together for the country.

Upon their arrival, Karl and Mr. Pollunder are met at the door by Mr. Pollunder's daughter Clara who informs her father that Mr. Green has also arrived. Though Mr. Pollunder is noticeably upset by this news, he does not express his displeasure directly to Mr. Green. Before long, they gather around the dinner table where Mr. Green relates his surprise that Karl's uncle let him go away to the country.

As the meal proceeds, Karl grows increasingly upset by Mr. Green's behavior. He fixates on his gestures and finds himself appalled by his domineering character. As the meal winds down, Karl realizes that he has scarcely eaten. To compensate, he shovels food down his throat and winds up grossly full and in a stupor. After Mr. Green and Mr. Pollunder adjourn to a living room table, Clara leads Karl upstairs and points out the room where he is meant to stay.

Karl wants to take a look at his room, but Clara asks him to wait. In spite of her request, Karl enters the room and sits on the ledge. Clara enters the room screaming and nearly pushes him out the window. Karl tries to seize her hands, but she breaks free and pins him to the couch. She threatens to box his ears, but finally lets him go, telling him that he is still welcome to visit her room.

Karl wants to go back to his uncle's house and decides to ask Mr. Pollunder for assistance. When he leaves his room, he realizes how big and dark the house is. He feels hopelessly lost until an old servant with a lantern finds him on the stairs. The servant leads Karl down to the living room and agrees to wait for him. Mr. Pollunder and Mr. Green are still engaged in conversation. Karl sits down by Mr. Pollunder's legs and tells him that he's worried that he may have offended his uncle, asking his host for permission to leave.

Mr. Pollunder agrees to help him get a train back to New York, but Mr. Green reveals that he has a message for him which he is not allowed to deliver until midnight. Though Karl is eager to go, he decides to ascend to Clara's room where he will spend the remaining half hour before midnight.

Karl has the servant take him back to Clara's room, where her demeanor has greatly improved. She asks Karl to play the piano and though it is late, he agrees. After playing two songs, Mack appears unexpectedly and gives Karl a round of applause. When the clock strikes midnight, Karl is met out in the hall by an agitated Mr. Green who has a letter from Karl's uncle. It states that Karl is not invited to return since he acted against his uncle's wishes. Mr. Green also has Karl's box of belongings which Schubal had apparently found on the ship and returned to Karl's uncle. Karl takes the news with surprising strength and asks to be escorted outside.

After a short walk, Karl finds a small inn where he asks for the cheapest room available. He is escorted up to the top floor and brought to a room that two men are already occupying with no spare beds. Concerned for his safety, Karl decides to introduce himself to the men. One of the men ignores him and rolls over, but the other introduces his friend as Robinson, an Irishman, and himself as Delamarch, a Frenchman. Following the introductions, Delamarch blows out Karl's candle and they all go to sleep.

The following day, Karl is woken up by Robinson and Delamarche who suggest that he let them sell his suit. Without fully understanding, Karl allows his suit to be taken by the two strangers who return almost immediately with half a dollar. Then the Landlady arrives and kicks them all out. They walk together along the street until they find a place to eat. After lunch, Karl pays for the meal and they continue to walk north, away from the city. When Karl says that he'd like to return to New York, Delamarche insists that they go to Butterford first, as there are jobs available. Karl agrees and walks with the men until the sun starts to set, and they settle on top of a grassy hill near the Hotel Occidental. Karl volunteers to go to the hotel and bring back some dinner.

Karl enters the hotel and is struck by the noise and the general state of chaos. He finally gets the attention of a woman who takes him back toward the kitchen and asks him what he wants. After giving him bacon, bread and beer, she suggests that he and his friends stay in the hotel. Karl declines, but agrees to come back the next morning to pay for the food and return the empty basket.

When Karl returns, he finds his companions asleep and the contents of his previously locked box strewn around the ground. Understandably upset, Karl berates his companions and says that he will be spending the night at the hotel. When Robinson and Delamarche are done eating, they threaten Karl, suggesting that they might beat him up and take more of his belongings. It is at this point that a waiter from the hotel arrives and says that he was asked to retrieve the basket. Karl says that he will be returning to the hotel with the waiter. As he gathers his things, he realizes that he can't find the photograph of his parents. He and the waiter search Robinson and Delamarche's pockets, but they are not able to find the photograph. Finally they leave and go back to the Hotel Occidental.

Upon entering the hotel, Karl is taken to the Manageress who finishes a dictation to her secretary and then expresses delight in seeing Karl. She asks if he is German. Her name is Grete Mitzelbach and she is from Vienna. The Manageress asks if he'd like a job at the hotel and Karl says that he would. She tells Karl that he can stay in the room connected to her bedroom for the evening and then if he wishes, he can work as a lift-boy and sleep in the quarters designated for them. Karl agrees to the situation and settles himself on the couch. Before he falls asleep, he hears a knock on the door. It is the Manageress' secretary, Therese, who engages him in conversation and then agrees to wake him up the following morning.

Though the Manageress wants Karl to take his first day to explore town, he is eager to begin his new job. After getting fitted for a uniform, he situates himself in the dormitory designated for lift-boys and begins his shift. Karl is trained by a boy named Giocomo. He works diligently at his post, and despite inadequate sleep, he does not complain. Throughout the month and a half that Karl works as a lift-boy, he spends as much time as possible with Therese. She shares a lot about her life including the last day she spent with her mother. Karl eventually begins taking grammar lessons from her.

But his troubles begin when another lift-boy named Rennel, for whom Karl had filled in on a previous occasion, tells Karl that a man named Delamarche had inquired about him. Though Karl is committed to staying away from his past cohorts, he is forced to act when Robinson enters the hotel drunk and gets sick over the banister. Working quickly, Karl takes him up to the dormitory and lets him pass out on one of the beds. When he returns to his post, he finds that his lift is in use. When it returns, he is told that guests were waiting to ride and the Head Waiter had seen Karl's neglected post.

Karl goes to the Head Waiter's office where he finds him talking to the Head Porter. He is ignored at first, but when the Head Waiter finally acknowledges him, he is enraged and dismisses Karl from his duties. Though Karl had only left his post for two minutes, the Head Waiter refuses to listen to any excuse. Then the Head Porter reproaches Karl for not greeting him every time they pass one another. Karl claims that he does greet the Head Porter, but since they cross paths so many times throughout the course of a day, he thought it inappropriate to engage in a formal greeting every time.

The Head Waiter calls the Manageress and tells her of Karl's dismissal. Then the Head Porter whispers in his colleague's ear, suggesting that Karl sneaks out every night to drink and spend time with women. Karl denies these false accusations, but he is quickly quieted. Before long, Therese and the Manageress come to the Head Waiter's office to hear the accusations first hand. The Head Porter brutally clutches Karl's arm. The situation grows worse when another lift-boy named Best arrives and tells the Head Waiter that Karl had brought a drunk man into the dormitory. The accusations get worse when it is suggested that Karl had stolen alcohol to get Robinson drunk, and by the end of the interrogation, even the Manageress believes that Karl should be dismissed. Though Karl is upset by all these false and slanted claims, he silently accepts his fate.

Before she leaves, the Manageress sends Therese to pack Karl's box and provides him with a note that will allow him to lodge in a nearby establishment. Karl is then dragged by the Head Porter into his office where he physically and verbally abuses him. But as the Head Porter searches through Karl's pockets, Karl slips out of the office and runs into the street. Once outside, he sees Robinson being carried on a stretcher by lift boys. He is bandaged up and being taken toward a taxi cab. Robinson asks why Karl had left him alone for so long. Karl doesn't answer, but jumps in the taxi with Robinson and gets driven away from the Hotel Occidental.

The taxi stops at a suburban residence. When Robinson confirms that they are at the right location, Karl gets out of the car and starts to walk away. He is stopped by the taxi driver who demands the fee for the taxi ride. As Karl begins to explain that he has no money, two police officers, who had been parked up the street, start to make their way toward the taxi. At this point, a shout is heard from the balcony above them, and Karl looks up to see Delamarche, peering through opera glasses at the whole scene. He puts them down and makes his way to the street where he pays the taxi driver what is owed. The police ask Karl for his papers, but since he left so hastily he has nothing to produce. He admits that he had worked at the Hotel Occidental but was dismissed only an hour before. Though Delamarche tries to convince the officers that they should leave Karl with him, they seem intent on returning him to the hotel. When the situation does not seem favorable, Karl flees down the road, barely eluding the pursuing officers. After a circuitous chase, he turns down a side street where he is pulled into an alcove by Delamarche who keeps him hidden until the officers pass.

Karl follows Delamarche back to the building where he is staying, and they walk up an enormous number of stairs to the top apartment. Robinson is lying against the door when they arrive. Delamarche peers through the key hole and decides that it's all right to enter. When they enter the apartment, Delamarche introduces Karl to Brunelda. Responding to her wish to take a bath and cool off, Delamarche pushes Karl and Robinson out on the balcony where they lie down and go to sleep.

Karl wakes up later that evening. Robinson asks him to move over so he can grab the food he had stored beneath Karl's seat. He takes out a can of sardines, some bread and a few cigarettes and starts to tell Karl about how he is treated like a dog by Delamarche and Brunelda. But when Karl asks why he stands for such treatment, Robinson gets defensive, suggesting that Brunelda is a wonderful woman and that Karl too will stand for the same treatment. Though Karl states emphatically that he will not stand for the same treatment, Robinson refuses to believe him.

Robinson tells Karl about how they came to live with Brunelda, and how they worked as beggars until they met her. She took a liking to Delamarche and brought them home to live with her. At the time Brunelda had a lot of servants, but she wanted to live alone with Delamarche so she fired them all, and decreed Robinson the sole servant. Robinson explains how his health began to fail under the burden of the household responsibilities, and that Delamarche had suggested that they get Karl to take his place. Insisting that he would never agree to such a thing, Karl makes a move for the door but is stopped by Robinson who instigates a minor scuffle. When the scuffle ends, and they are nursing their respective wounds, Brunelda and Delamarche step out onto the balcony to watch the procession that Robinson and Karl had not noticed. Delamarche asks the neighbors what the procession is about, and learns that there is an election for judge the following day and they are backing one of the candidates.

While they all stare down at the procession, Karl starts to plan his escape. As he considers the most effective route out, he notices Robinson whispering into Delamarche's ear, likely about Karl's intentions to leave. But when the procession becomes more raucous, and Delamarche, Brunelda and Robinson become increasingly occupied by the activities, Karl sneaks inside with the intention of leaving the flat. Upon discovering that the flat door is locked, he finds some knives and tries to pry the lock open. Before he can do this, he is discovered by Delamarche who leaps on him. Karl opts not to use the knives as defense and instead employs the fighting skills learned at the hotel to ward off Delamarche's blows and immobilize him with his arms. But just when he detains Delamarche, he is attacked by Robinson who throws him hard against the wall. He remains under attack by Robinson and Delamarche until a blow to the head knocks him out.

When Karl wakes up, it is night again and everyone is sleeping. There is a wet bandage on his head and he goes out to the balcony to see whether the dampness is blood. While he is outside, he has a conversation with the neighbor, Joseph Mendel, who is studying on the adjacent balcony. He tells Karl that he despises Brunelda and Delamarche. Karl asks him about his studies and he tells him that he works all day at the local market and studies all night. Finally Karl takes leave of Joseph and goes inside where he falls asleep.

The novel continues the following day at a street corner where Karl is looking at a placard advertising employment at the Oklahoma Theatre. The traveling theatre company is currently in Clayton which is about three hours away. Karl checks his money supply and decides to take a train up to Clayton.

When he gets off the train, he is greeted by the sound of blaring trumpets. Though it is certainly unusual, Karl accepts it as a sign of a working theatre and starts walking toward the sound. As he gets closer, he sees a number of women on different pedestals each blowing a trumpet. Karl talks to a man and a woman who ask him if he would find out where prospective employees should inquire. When Karl walks further in, he realizes that one of the trumpeteers is an old acquaintance named Fanny. She lets him play her trumpet and is astonished at how good he sounds. He suggests that he might look into working as a trumpet player as he heads off to enlist.

Karl is quickly greeted by the staff manager. Karl asks if he should wave the couple and their child on, and the manager assures him that everyone is welcome. When Karl makes it to the gate, he waves the couple on and sees a new load of potential employees emerging from the train. He hurries back to get in the employment line. When everyone starts to pull out their papers, Karl remembers that he doesn't have his. He hopes that this will not be an issue and decides to get the initial proceedings over with as soon as he can. The staff manager asks if there are any engineers in line and Karl steps forward.

Karl goes to the engineering bureau where he admits that he has no papers and that he's not an engineer yet. They send him to two different departments where he is finally accepted. But when asked his name, Karl is reluctant to divulge this information and says instead that his name is Negro.

Karl is eventually led to another area where he informs some inquiring individuals that he has been taken on as an actor but is not certain he is suited to the job. They ask him what his interests are and he says that he wants to be an engineer. They conclude that he might be better off working in some sort of technical capacity, a notion which Karl accepts. When he gets his label indicating that he has been taken on as a technical worker, he asks if he can go see Fanny. He is told that the trumpet players have been taken to the next site on a recruiting trip, but he will see them again in Oklahoma.

Soon, Karl finds himself at a reception for new employees, where he is fed well-cooked meat and served wine. While everyone is eating, Karl spots Giocomo from the Hotel Occidental. They greet each other and vow to stay together after the meal. The Staff Manager addresses them and says that they need to board the train. Karl and Giocomo sit next to each other on the train and get reacquainted. The novel ends with Karl looking out the window at the stunning scenery and reflecting on the vast size of the United States.

LIST OF CHARACTERS IN

Amerika

Karl Rossmann is the primary character and the first one the reader encounters. He is a German boy who takes a boat to America to avoid a scandal. He lives for a time with his uncle, a Senator, before he is expelled from his house. He has various adventures with a Frenchman named Delamarche and an Irishman named Robinson. He ends up working in the Oklahoma Theater where he is reunited with a friend from his days at the Hotel Occidental.

Senator Edward Joseph is Karl's uncle. He meets Karl on the boat and invites him to stay at his home in New York. He eventually kicks him out when Karl disobeys his request.

The Stoker is a worker on the ship who feels that he is discriminated against by Mr. Schubal. Karl tries to help him, but the Captain is not sympathetic to the Stoker's case.

Mr. Schubal is a worker on the ship who defends himself against the Stoker's claims that he has been discriminatory.

The Captain is in charge of the ship where Karl meets his uncle.

Mr. Pollunder is a friend of Karl's uncle. He invites Karl to his house to meet his daughter.

Mr. Green is a friend of Karl's uncle. He tells Karl that his uncle has expelled him from his New York home.

Clara Pollunder is Mr. Pollunder's daughter. She is engaged to Mr. Mack.

Mr. Mack is Karl's horseback riding teacher. He is engaged to Clara.

Robinson is an Irishman who travels with Delamarche and Karl. He ends up working as a servant for Delamarche and Brunelda.

Delamarche is a Frenchman who travels with Robinson and Karl. He is a swindler who manipulates Robinson into becoming his servant and attempts to do the same thing to Karl.

Giocomo met Karl at the Hotel Occidental. He is reunited with Karl at the end of the novel when the Oklahoma Theater employs them both.

The Manageress (Grete Mitzelbach) gets Karl a job at the Hotel Occidental.

Therese is the Manageress' secretary. She and Karl are friendly while he is an employee at the hotel.

Rennel is an employee at the Hotel Occidental.

The Head Waiter (Isbary) is responsible for firing Karl from the Hotel Occidental.

The Head Porter (Feodor) joins with the Head Waiter in the effort to berate and ultimately fire Karl from the hotel.

Best is an employee at the Hotel Occidental.

Brunelda is a rich woman who takes Delamarche into her home and makes Robinson her servant.

Fanny works in the Oklahoma Theater.

Amerika

KLAUS MANN ON *AMERIKA*

[Klaus Mann is the son of Nobel Prize winning author Thomas Mann. He was once Director of the Berlin State Theater, and is often remembered for his autobiography *The Turning Point*. In this excerpt, Mann speaks on the influences that helped shape the novel.]

The most extensive journey he ever made took place wholly in his mind. The goal of his bold excursion was the United States. His friends were highly surprised when he confided to them his secret—that he was going to write a novel entitled *Amerika*: in fact, he had already begun.

"What do you know about America?" they asked. And he answered, cheerfully: "I know the autobiography of Benjamin Franklin, and I always admired Walt Whitman, and I like the Americans because they are healthy and optimistic." He imagined that all Americans wore a perpetual smile. Later, in the years of his fatal disease, he met in a sanatorium several Americans who quite often grumbled and complained. He was deeply disappointed. But when he conceived his novel *Amerika*, in 1913, he knew no Americans at all and understood very little English. His only sources of information were the few books he had read—and his own poetic imagination.

He seemed unusually cheerful and confident while working on *Amerika*. His friends were pleased to notice that his looks and mood had improved almost miraculously. His relative optimism, however, did not entirely protect him from qualms and scruples. He was at that time reading, or re-reading, several novels by Dickens, and made the following remarks in his diary:

"Dickens, *Copperfield*. 'The Stoker,' a plain imitation of Dickens: even more so than the planned novel." (The first chapter of the America novel was published as a special little volume, called 'The Stoker', before the novel appeared.) ... My intention was, as I now see, to write a Dickens novel, enriched by the sharper lights which I took from our modern times, and by the pallid ones I would have found in my own interior.— Dickens' wealth and naive, sweeping power: but, consequently, moments of horrible weakness ... The impression of the senseless whole is barbaric—a barbarism which I was able to avoid thanks to my decadence..."

Strangely enough, in Kafka's mind the figure and the works of Dickens were vitally connected with the American atmosphere and landscape. It was not Dickens' biting satire on America, in *Martin Chuzzlewit*, that lay behind this odd identification. The picture that Kafka cherished was of a fatherly genius called Charles Dickens being welcomed to New York with wild enthusiasm by thousands of his American readers. Kafka often described to his friends the hilarious spectacle of all that exuberant public jammed on the dock, eagerly awaiting a new chapter of *David Copperfield*, waving and shouting as the boat with its literary treasure slowly pulls in.

As to his own novel, *Amerika*, he was far from accurate when he called it an "imitation of Dickens." For the resemblance to Dickens is only accidental and superficial—while the differences between the sentimental or humorous circumstantiality of Dickens' style and Kafka's visionary precision are basic and essential.

—Klaus Mann, "Preface," *Amerika*, by Franz Kafka (New York, Schocken Books, 1946): pp: xxvi-xxvii.

LIENHARD BERGEL ON *AMERIKA* AND ITS MEANING

[Lienhard Bergel was a scholar and a critic whose essays have appeared in such volumes as *The Kafka Problem* and *Franz Kafka Today*. In this excerpt, Bergel suggests that it is the realistic nature of the novel that makes it successful.]

AMONG Kafka's novels, *Amerika* has received least attention and least critical approval. The book is usually regarded merely as

Kafka's first effort in the novel form, a trial run that remained largely unsuccessful. The only merit critics have found in the book has been that it foreshadowed his "greater" novels: fragments here and there seemed to be embryonic *Trials* and embryonic *Castles*. Compared with the other novels, *Amerika* seemed old-fashioned; as one critic put it, the "dream-distortions" that make the later novels so fascinating, so "expressionistic," are missing; the public associates Kafka with the unexpected, the weird and fantastic, and is disappointed to find a novel that is fairly traditional in form and makes sense rather easily.

Against this point of view, the reverse may be argued: Kafka is artistically most successful where his technique is least bizarre and most conventional. Kafka reaches his highest achievements in the fable, a framework that permits him to write a story which, at least on the surface, does not differ essentially from the traditional fictional forms of realistic provenience. "A Hunger-Artist," for instance, is at first glance a fully coherent brief biography devoid of dream-distortions; similarly, "The Burrow" conforms outwardly to the traditional animal story form. Where Kafka distorts, he is frequently, not always, fumbling artistically; the emotional experiences that provide the raw material for his work have not undergone sufficient esthetic transformation: "the man who suffers and the mind which creates" are still too closely identified. It is therefore not surprising that Kafka's artistic failures have evoked most discussion: here is grist for the mills of psychoanalytic and existentialist interpretations. It is an indirect confirmation of the artistic solidity of *Amerika* that the novel has proved comparatively impervious to interpretations of this kind (which may be one reason for its neglect) and equally unrewarding for sociological investigations; a distinguished Marxist critic found the book "disappointing" and "incomprehensible."

In *Amerika*, Kafka resorts to the oldest form of realistic fiction, the novel of adventure, and its modern offspring, the novel of education, joining with these the traditional motif of the simpleton who is sent out to experience the world. Upon this inherited framework he imposes a typically modern novelistic situation, the hero between two continents, the emigrant from the old to the new world. Thus a firm realistic structure is established which makes it possible for Kafka to unfold to the fullest his unique artistic ability to raise ordinary human situations to the symbolic level, and which makes it unnecessary for him to resort to the fantastic and absurd in the scaffolding of the fable.

—Lienhard Bergel, "*Amerika*: Its Meaning," *Franz Kafka Today*, eds.: Angel Flores and Homer Swander (Madison, The University of Wisconsin Press, 1958): pp: 117-118.

HEINZ POLITZER ON THE INNOCENCE OF KARL ROSSMANN

[Heinz Politzer was Professor Emeritus at Berkeley before his death in 1978. Remembered as one of the foremost Kafka scholars, he was the author of *Franz Kafka: Parable and Paradox*. In this excerpt, Politzer discusses the uncertainties and possibilities that surround the novel.]

As early as July 10, 1912, Kafka wrote a letter to Max Brod containing some vague allusions to the story which he later was to call *Der Verschollene* ("The Boy Who Was Never More Heard Of") and which was published posthumously as *Amerika*. The letter read, in part:

The novel is as great as if it had been sketched across the whole sky (also as colorless and as uncertain as this day), and I get entangled in the first sentence that I want to write. But I have found out already that I must not be deterred by the hopelessness of what I have written and I profited considerably yesterday by this experience (B, 96).

On September 30, 1915, be compared in his diaries the hero of this novel, with which he still seemed to be occupied, and the hero of *The Trial*: "Rossmann and K., the guiltless and the guilty, both executed without distinction in the end, the guiltless one with a gentler hand, more pushed aside than struck down" (*DII*, 132). Two years later, on October 8, 1917, while reading Dickens' *David Copperfield*, he commented on the first chapter of his story:

> "The Stoker," a sheer imitation of Dickens, the projected novel even more so. The story of the trunk, the boy who delights and charms everyone, the menial labor, his sweetheart on the country estate, the dirty houses, *et al.*, but above all the method. It was my intention, as I now see, to write a Dickens novel, but enhanced by the sharper lights I should have taken from the times, and the duller ones I should have gotten from myself.... [Dickens] gives one a barbaric impression because the whole does not make sense, a barbarism that I, thanks to my weakness and wiser for my being his epigone, have been able to avoid (DII, 188, 189).

We do not know the name Kafka would have given his novel eventually. Nor do we possess any certainty about Karl Rossmann's ultimate fate. For Kafka's plan to have him "executed" is contradicted by Brod, who remembers, "From what he told me, I know that the incomplete chapter about the nature theatre of Oklahoma ... was intended to be the concluding chapter of the work and should end on a note of reconciliation" (277).[1] Kafka's natural hesitation in deciding upon conclusive endings for his stories has, in the case of *Der Verschollene*, an outward and objective reason. He had begun to write the novel sometime in 1911 or 1912, in any case before the breakthrough, and the meeting with F. B. in August 1912. Thus he had to apply the vastly enhanced and refined creative powers that this crisis had produced in him to the completion of a plan whose derivative character became more and more clear to him and whose vastness was, as he early recognized, imperiled by his uncertainty about it. Indeed, he seems very soon to have become aware of the incompatibility of the material at hand with the new means now at his disposal.

The diary entry of September 25, 1912, is followed by the final version, still untitled, of "The Stoker" (*DI*, 330). Its appearance here leaves us uncertain whether he composed this first chapter of *Der Verschollene* after the breakthrough or only recast older material to fit a new style. Although he continued his work on the novel proper, Kafka acknowledged the independence of "The Stoker" by agreeing to its publication in Kurt Wolff's series *Der Jüngste Tag*, where it appeared in May 1913. His decision to release the manuscript may be taken as an indication that he had given up the hope of finishing the longer story of which it was a part. He treated "The Stoker" as he was to treat the parable "Before the Law," which in his will he condemned as part of *The Trial*, while he allowed it to "survive" independently as one of the *Country Doctor* stories. Just as "Before the Law" contains in essence a statement about Kafka's relation to the world of metaphysics, so does "The Stoker" in an exemplary way probe his attitude toward the physical world, even though it was a reality he had never experienced.

NOTE

1. Numbers without letters refer to the 1946 American edition entitled *Amerika*. As will be seen from the following interpretation, especially pp. 124–129 and p. 162, the name *Der Verschollene* seems more appropriate to me. Wherever the context permitted me to do so, I have used this title instead of *Amerika*.

—Heinz Politzer, "*Der Verschollene*: The Innocence of Karl Rossmann," *Franz Kafka: Parable and Paradox*, (Ithaca: Cornell University Press, 1962): pp. 116-118.

CALVIN S. HALL AND RICHARD E. LIND ON PARENTAL FIGURES

[Calvin S. Hall has been the director of the Institute of Dream Research. He has published numerous books including *The Meaning of Dreams* and *Dreams, Life and Literature: A Study of Franz Kafka*. Richard E. Lind has studied and worked with Calvin Hall. His publications include *The Seeking Self: The Search for Self Improvement and the Creation of Personal Suffering* and *Devil's Due*. In this excerpt, Hall and Lind discuss the impact of the mother and father figures in the novel.]

The male authorities in *Amerika* divide into two categories: those who are hostile to Karl and those who are helpful. The first category consists of Karl's two "bosses"—the Head Porter and the Head Waiter—in the hotel where he works for a short time. Out of 22 encounters with them, 19 are unfriendly, and in all of these 19 Karl is the victim. The second category consists of older men, e.g., Karl's uncle and his uncle's friend, Pollander. With them Karl has few aggressive interactions (the proportion is .25), and he is the recipient of considerable friendliness from them (the proportion is .71).

The only female authority with whom Karl interacts is the Manageress of the hotel. She is almost always friendly to Karl, 19 friendly versus 2 unfriendly. So is Therese, a fellow employee, and Karl is also friendly to her. The situation is quite different for Karl's social interactions with another peer female, Clara. With her he has more hostile relations, 15 aggressions versus six friendly. In these encounters, there is a give and take although Clara is more apt to be the aggressor, nine aggressions against Karl versus six by Karl against her. Moreover, her aggressions are more violent and physical than his. She is a "masculine" woman. It is interesting that Karl's relations with Mr. Mack, Clara's fiance, are exclusively friendly.

The analysis so far shows that there are good "father" figures who try to help the immigrant boy who has been sent to the United States by his parents for having made a servant girl pregnant, and had "father" figures who are cruel to Karl. Peer females are also divided into friendly and hostile types but the one "mother" figure is almost uniformly helpful. Spilka (1963) observes that the Manageress and the Chief Waiter are in league against Karl and that this reflects Kafka's feelings about his own mother and father. It is true that after befriending Karl the Manageress lets him be discharged but the charges against Karl are so serious that she cannot overlook them.

Several characters do not fit the foregoing analysis. One of these is the Stoker on the ship by which Karl travels to New York. Karl befriends him eight times—there is no hostility—but the Stoker is ambivalent toward Karl, five aggressions and five friendlinesses toward Karl.

The pattern of aggression and friendliness with the two

mechanics, Delamarche and Robinson, whom Karl meets on the road and with whom he travels, and later lives, and with Brunelda, Delamarche's mistress, are also different from the other characters in the book. With these three characters, Karl has 55 aggressive and 45 friendly interactions. Karl is the aggressor 29 times and the victim 26 times. He is the befriender 16 times and he is befriended 29 times. These characters like the others in the book except for Clara and the Stoker befriend Karl, but they also give and receive a lot of aggression.

> —Calvin S. Hall and Richard E. Lind, "Content Analysis of Kafka's Novels," *Dreams, Life and Literature: A Study of Franz Kafka*, (Chapel Hill: The University of North Carolina Press, 1970): pp. 63-65.

EVELYN TORTON BECK ON THE DRAMATIC IN KAFKA'S WORK

[Evelyn Torton Beck has been a prominent translator and literary scholar. Her translations have appeared in *Commentary* and *The New Yorker*. In this excerpt, Beck speaks about the novel's inability to successfully mix dramatic elements within the narrative prose.]

Although far more successful than anything else Kafka wrote before "The Judgment" *Der Verschollene* is not as powerful or convincing as the later work. As a whole, it does not apply dramatic method to narrative prose; it does, however, include many sections that bear the mark of the later style.[2] The initial meeting between Karl and the stoker (brought about by Karl's chance knock on the cabin door) is an especially good example of a "staged" scene, which, like the drama, is enacted in a limited space, develops character and action by means of terse dialogue, and is punctuated by large, significant gestures: "'But then I must go up and see about it at once,' said Karl, looking round for the way out. 'You just stay where you are,' said the man, giving him a push with one hand on the chest, quite roughly, so that he fell back on the bunk again. 'But why?' asked Karl in exasperation.

'Because there's no point in it,' said the man" (*Am* 5–6).[3] The menace inherent in this situation (Karl is essentially imprisoned in the cabin of a total stranger) is not analyzed by the author, but conveyed solely by means of word, gesture, and tone. Similarly, the stoker's self-imposed "trial" in the captain's office, which builds on the effects of the previous scene, is constructed like a melodrama in which mystery and suspense are introduced and embellished (Can the ineffectual stoker triumph over his powerful enemy, the hated Schubal?), only to be resolved unexpectedly with a great theatrical flourish (the stoker's case is completely overshadowed by Uncle Jakob's finding his nephew Karl).[4]

Begun sometime in early 1912, reworked between late 1912 and 1914, and finally abandoned in 1915 or 1916, *Der Verschollene* spans the years of transition and continues well into the later period.[5] The first chapter, "The Stoker" (published independently in *Der Jüngste Tag*, May, 1913), appeared in the *Diaries* on September 25, 1912, only a few days after "The Judgment," while the next five chapters were completed by mid-November 1912. A substantial portion of Chapter 7 was written (though not completed) in late November of that same year; there is a large gap in time between it and what was probably to have been the last chapter, "The Nature Theater of Oklahoma."[6] In addition to these, only two fragments of intervening material remain.

NOTES

2. Politzer (*Parable and Paradox*, p. 125) describes Karl's seduction by Johanna as an "early example of Kafka's mature prose style."

3. "'Da muss ich aber doch gleich hinaufschaun', sagte Karl und sah sich um, wie er hinauskommen könnte. 'Bleiben Sie nur', sagte der Mann, und stiess ihn mit einer Hand gegen die Brust, geradezu rauh, ins Bett zurück. 'Warum denn?' fragte Karl ärgerlich. 'Weil es keinen Sinn hat', sagte der Mann" (*A* 13).

4. Other staged scenes, all confined to a single setting, include the dinner at Mr. Pollunder's, Karl's encounter with Klara, Karl's

"trial" at the Hotel Occidental, Karl's attempted escape at Brunelda's, and especially Fragment I, Brunelda's bath, a scene in which the main character (Brunelda) is presented only as a voice and a force, while in the foreground her "slaves" (Karl and Robinson) rush frantically around the room trying to serve and appease her.

For a detailed discussion of the function of gesture and costume in this novel, see Jahn, "Kafka und die Anfänge des Kinos"; and idem, *Kafkas Roman "Der Verschollene."* In his discussion of *Der Verschollene* Jahn divides the novel into self-contained units (which he calls *Handlungszentren* [centers of action or plot]) whose structure corresponds to the individual acts of a play.

5. See Pasley and Wagenbach, "Datierung sämtlicher Texte," in *Kafka Symposion*, by Born et al., pp. 62–63; and Jürgen Born, Nom 'Urteil' zum *Prozess*: Zu Kafkas Leben und Schaffen in den Jahren 1912–1914," *ZDP* 86 (1967): 186–96.

6. H. Uyttersprot, *Eine Neue Ordnung der Werke Kafkas? Zu Struktur von "Der Prozess" und "Amerika"* (Antwerp, 1957), p. 73, suggests that the Nature Theater was not meant to be the final one, and that a chapter describing Karl's death was to follow.

—Evelyn Torton Beck, "The dramatic in Kafka's work to 1914," *Kafka and the Yiddish Theater: Its impact on his work*, (Madison: The University of Wisconsin Press, 1971): pp. 122-24.

HEINZ HILLMANN ON THE OKLAHOMA THEATRE

[Heinz Hillmann has been essayist and German literary scholar. His publications include *F.K.: Dichtungstheorie und Dichtungsgestalt*. In this excerpt, Hillmann speaks on the role of The Oklahoma Theater in the novel.]

The Oklahoma Theater is a society which develops people into artists and thus, in every respect, the antithesis of the American system. The individual is not a function of society—rather, society is a function of the individual. This antithesis is flawed to some extent. Certain problems, for example, that of property relations, do not seem to have been solved, even though Kafka starts out from the assumption that the individual member of the Oklahoma Theater society is not endowed with property (in exactly the same way as he was to do later in his plan for a propertyless proletariat). The administration which organizes that society, although humane, perpetuates the division of labor and does not enable society as a whole to organize itself. These contradictions and gaps cannot be evaluated unequivocally, since the chapter is incomplete. My interpretation of this chapter is equally tentative. I have only suggested a hypothesis which is plausible in certain respects, given Kafka's biography. There is no sense in laying down one's own line of Kafka interpretation (as critics so often do) on the basis of the uncompleted Oklahoma chapter.

Why Kafka neither carries through his project to design an alternative system, nor develops a whole series of experimental attempts needs explanation. The usual one (Kafka's petit-bourgeois background and consequent lack of perspective) has only a limited validity since other scions of the petite bourgeoisie, notably Brecht, acted differently. It is probable that a thesis as developed by the authority, applies to Kafka: the individual within a repressive system views himself as the one failure among a group of people who are more successful. Kafka described this attitude in the "Letter to his Father" when he characterized his father as the "paying enemy" of the employees and then differentiated between himself (who could not bear this situation because of his sensitivity and lack of self confidence) and the others (who could cope with it because most of them had "excellent nerves." (*H*, 187/*DF*, 162). Thus, Kafka understood himself as a peculiar case, as a deviation from the norm rather than as an individual case to whom what is valid for others generally also applied. Such a self-evaluation has considerable consequences for the writer who needs the assumption that his experience has some kind of general validity. If my experiences in the social system (be it Prague or America) are also yours, then there is something wrong with the system. In which case it is worth imagining an alternative system for both our sakes. If, however, a writer assumes that he is an exception, then the business of imagining an alternative system will issue in the blueprint for a world for a minority, a world for those who are too weak to cope. Which is exactly what happens in the Oklahoma chapter.

The conception of Karl, however, shows Kafka's intent to evolve the writer's assumption of general validity. Karl is, for all his sensitivity, a young man with strong nerves. In this respect he does not belong to the minority of those who are too weak to cope (among whom Kafka counted himself). Kafka is not simply enquiring whether his own ego, if it is well equipped, can withstand the world. Rather, he is asking, much more generally, whether the American world is not so constituted as inevitably to destroy even those with stronger nerves. He is investigating the system by analyzing its effects on different people. He does not just put himself through the system, he uses other figures in order to discover whether he really is so singular a case after all.

—Heinz Hillmann, "*Amerika*: Literature as a Problem-solving Game," *The Kafka Debate: New Perspectives For Our Time*, ed. Angel Flores (New York: Gordian Press, 1977): pp. 286-87.

RITCHIE ROBERTSON ON THE URBAN WORLD

[Ritchie Robertson has been a Fellow of Downing College in Cambridge. His published works include *Kafka: Judaism, Politics, and Literature*. In this excerpt, Robertson discusses the root of Kafka's interest in America.]

Kafka's interest in contemporary America owed little to imaginative literature and a great deal to personal contacts and non-fictional accounts. Several of his relations had emigrated to America and made good there. His cousin Otto (the son of Kafka's paternal uncle Philipp, a businessman in the Bohemian town of Kolín) had gone there in 1906, with no contacts and no knowledge of English, had got a job as porter in a corset-making company, and worked his way up to become its export-manager. Later he founded his own business, the Kafka Export

Corporation, and married into an American family. Otto's youngest brother, Franz (known in America as Frank), joined him in New York in 1909, and, after attending a private school there, became a clerk in the Kafka Export Corporation. In *Der Verschollene* Kafka seems to have combined details of their careers with some recollections of their brother Robert Kafka, a highly successful lawyer in Prague, who at the age of fourteen had been seduced by his parents' forty-year-old cook and fathered her son. Another cousin, Emil Kafka, had emigrated to America in 1904 and worked for the Sears Roebuck department store in Chicago. He is the 'E. K. aus Chicago' mentioned in Kafka's diary for 9 December (T 447), and the meeting with him probably helped to suggest the student Mendel who works in Montly's department store in *Der Verschollene*.

These real-life examples of success in America must have strengthened Kafka's feeling of being a stay-at-home and a failure. There were other, remoter examples, such as Thomas Alva Edison, who visited Prague in September 1911 and, with 1,200 patents to his name, impressed people as the very incarnation of American drive and ingenuity. Kafka copied into his diary for 11 November part of a newspaper interview in which Edison attributed the industrial development of Bohemia to the energy of emigrants returning from America (T 155). As Johannes Urzidil explains, Edison was probably thinking of one of his own closest colleagues, a Prague Jew named Kolben who returned to his native city and became a prominent industrialist. Since the Prague Jewish community was so small, Kafka would certainly have known of Kolben and found in him further grounds for self-reproach. The *Prager Tagblatt*, which Kafka read on most days, reported on American politics, and also gave much space to American technological developments in its Friday supplement 'Aus Technik und Industrie'.

From all these sources Kafka was aware of America as a country where everything was on a vaster scale than in Europe and where anyone could become rich with sufficient determination. This view is present in *Der Verschollene*, but superimposed on it is another, darker view of America as a society licensing the most ruthless exploitation of the disadvantaged, and using machinery to carry to extremes the process of dehumanization which Kafka had observed on his factory visits. He knew, for example, about the difficulties faced by 'greenhorns' or newly arrived immigrants: the Yiddish poems which Löwy recited on the occasion organized by Kafka in February 1912 included one by Rosenfeld describing the arrival of 'greenhorns' in New York. The slums on the East Side where immigrants clustered are twice referred to in *Der Verschollene* (V 97, 196), and the story Therese tells about her mother's death vividly conveys the misery of immigrants unable to find work or even shelter for the night.

—Ritchie Robertson, "The Urban World," *Kafka: Judaism, Politics, and Literature* (Oxford: Clarendon Press, 1985): pp. 47-48.

E.L. DOCTOROW ON *AMERIKA*

[E.L. Doctorow is one of the most distinguished novelists of our time. His novels include *Ragtime* and *Billy Bathgate*. In this excerpt, Doctorow speaks on the perception of the novel.]

In 1912, the twenty-nine-year-old Franz Kafka, a lifelong resident of Prague whose occasional travels had taken him no farther than Paris, decided to write a novel set in America. We might wonder why, except that the United States had by then clearly emerged as a world power and a focal point for universal aspiration. To a German-speaking Czech Jewish writer gravely aware of living in a deadeningly historicized world, the idea of a New World would have a certain scintillation. This was to be Kafka's first novel, and though he'd never been to America, he seemed confident that he could compensate for his ignorance by diligent research. According to his biographer Ernst Pawel, Kafka read American travel books, attended lectures, collected printed materials, and spoke with returning emigrants, all for the purpose of writing a realistic novel authenticated with "up-to-date" American detail.

We will always revere genius, but we only love it when it doesn't know itself. In Kafka's *Amerika* the Statue of Liberty greets transoceanic arrivals with a raised sword. The port of New York presumably has no ship berths; when young Karl Rossmann, Kafka's immigrant hero, debarks from his liner he is rowed to shore. Staying at an uncle's well-appointed Manhattan apartment, Karl lies flat in a bathtub the size of a room and is sprayed from numerous shower heads. His uncle is a "Senator" who seems to have no role in government, the usage connoting a titled rank, such as Count or Baron. When Karl leaves the city he runs into a strike of metal workers picketing in a suburb that suggests Scarsdale. He is a guest in a suburban home in which servants, in full livery, walk about the drafty castle-like corridors with huge candelabra held in both hands. Karl travels deeper into the country along highways implanted with towers from which police direct the traffic. Tilled farm fields have tenements rising from them. A country town, presumably in upstate New York, has a subway system. A hotel is staffed by a hierarchy of uniformed professionals of the servant class, from imperial headwaiters down to overworked bellhops. When people on the street are stopped by the police, they must show their identity papers.

Kafka wrote two drafts before he abandoned the manuscript, unfinished, which suggests self-admitted failure—but in what sense? The work places *Popular Mechanics* notions of modernity in a Central European landscape. Had he failed his intention to write a realistic novel, or had he failed his vision?

The vast foreign literature of the obsession with America offers, as exemplary authors of the genre, Tocqueville and Dickens who, like so many others, came across to see first hand the biggest news story of their time and went back to record their impressions. But there is a subgenre of American studies that, derived from secondary sources, is visionary, factually unreliable, exploitative, and sometimes ludicrous. In this category we find works as notable as Bertolt Brecht's *Arturo Ui*, a play set in the meat-packing quarter of Chicago, or his *Mahagonny*, which sings lyrically of a full moon over the state of Alabama (both works written before Brecht ever arrived on these shores), but also the German-language potboilers of Karl May, who wrote scores of widely read novels of the American Wild West without having ventured out of Saxony.

> —E.L. Doctorow, "Foreward," *Amerika*, by Franz Kafka (New York, Schocken Books, 1946): pp. ix-xi.

The Castle

The Castle, one of Kafka's three posthumously published novels, opens as the protagonist, known only as K., arrives in a village positioned beneath a looming Castle. K., who has been hired as a land surveyor, enters a nearby inn. Although there are no beds available, he is allowed to stay on a straw mattress on the floor. He falls asleep almost immediately, but is soon woken by the steward's son who tells him that he won't be allowed to stay unless he shows permission from the Count, as the inn is Castle property. K. tells the man, who's name is Schwarzer, that he is the land surveyor and has been appointed by the Count.

Although Schwarzer is skeptical, the Castle does have a record of K. As compensation for the confusion, K. is offered the landlord's room. The following day, he talks to the landlord who assures him that his room and board will be covered. K. decides to leave the inn and walk toward the Castle. En route, he runs into a school teacher with whom he has a brief conversation about the appearance of the Castle. K. asks for the teacher's address so he can call on him at some later time.

Fatigued and tired, K. keeps walking along a path that never seems to get closer to the Castle. It is snowing and he becomes desperate for rest and shelter. He opens a random cottage door and identifies himself as the land surveyor. Much to his surprise, the people inside are aware of him. In the comfort of the cottage, K. falls asleep. When he wakes up, he is told that he must leave. He agrees and starts along a path toward the Castle, which is covered in heavy snow. Finally, someone calls to him from a window and offers to take him to the inn by sleigh.

An older man named Gerstacker meets K. outside with a sleigh and though he is stricken by illness, he insists on taking K. back to the inn. When they make it back, K.'s assistants, Artur and Jeremias, are waiting for him. The three go to the taproom where they have beer and talk. K. tells his assistants that he'd like to go to the Castle first thing in the morning, and they remind him that he needs permission before he is allowed onto the

Castle grounds. K. asks his assistants to phone for permission. They come back moments later and reveal that permission was not granted. K. decides to phone the Castle himself, but he too is denied.

After K.'s call to the Castle, a messenger named Barnabas shows up with a letter acknowledging his position as land surveyor. It also says that he is supposed to report to the village council chairman. The letter indicates that Barnabas will be available to K. if he needs him. K. rereads the letter, fixating on the ambiguities of his status. Once he has finished, he talks again to Barnabas who reveals that his superior's name is Klamm. When Barnabas leaves, K. runs after him so he can inquire about other ways of communicating with Klamm and the Castle.

Because of the unsure footing, K. takes Barnabas' arm. As they walk, K. gets lost in his thoughts. When they finally stop, Barnabas reveals that he has brought K. to his home. K. follows the messenger inside and is introduced to his parents, as well as his sisters, Olga and Amalia. Olga discloses that she is going to the Gentleman's Inn, and K. asks if he can accompany her. When they arrive, K. finds the landlord and asks if he can spend the night there. His request is denied. K. starts to argue his case, but he stops upon realizing that Klamm is in the building and it might present an awkward situation if he were to be caught spending the night at an inn reserved exclusively for Castle employees.

The drinks at the Gentlemen's Inn are served by a woman named Frieda. K. asks her if she knows Mr. Klamm. Olga laughs at K.'s question, while Frieda leads him to a peephole where he can see Klamm sitting in a chair. As he peers at Klamm, she reveals that she is his mistress. Frieda puts a cork into the peephole, and K. follows her to the bar, where he asks if they might be able to speak in private. Frieda says they can and tells the servants to leave the taproom.

While Frieda is forcing everyone out, K. hears footsteps in the corridor and hides behind the counter. It is the landlord who arrives and asks Frieda where K. has gone. Though she is aware of K.'s presence, she doesn't reveal his whereabouts. When the landlords leaves, Frieda turns off the light and joins K. beneath the counter where they embrace in the darkness. After many hours beneath the counter, Klamm calls for Frieda and she tells him that she's with the surveyor. Surprised by her response, K. climbs out from beneath the counter and finds his assistants and Olga waiting for him. The assistants claim to have been in the taproom all night. As the sun starts to rise, Frieda, K. and the assistants leave the Gentlemen's inn and walk to another inn by the bridge where Frieda lives.

K. spends the rest of the evening and most of the next day in bed. When he finally rises, he is waited on by Frieda and his assistants. K. grows quickly annoyed by his assistants and asks them to go away so he can spend some time alone with Frieda. They reluctantly comply, and K. and Frieda are left alone to embrace. Later, K. has his first conversation with the Landlady of the inn.

When K. expresses his desire to speak with Klamm, the Landlady and Frieda protest vehemently, claiming that a discussion between the two would be impossible. The argument leads to a discussion of K. and Frieda's place at the inn. K. claims that he is not dependent on a room at the Landlady's inn as he has an open invitation to stay at the messenger Barnabas' house. Frieda and the Landlady react to the mention of this name, suggesting that he and his family are disrespectable. Their conversation ends as K. leaves for an appointment with the Council Chairman.

The Chairman, described as "a friendly fat clean-shaven man," is sick when K. arrives and speaks to him from his bed. K. reads him the letter from Klamm. The Chairman says that despite the letter, K.'s presence is a mistake and that there is no need for a surveyor. K. expresses his surprise and displeasure, to which the Chairman explains that the Count's administration is so vast that there are multiple departments issuing orders at the same time, each one not always aware of the other. He goes on to emphasize that errors are extremely rare, but in this case, he believes to know the reason behind it.

The Chairman asks his wife Mizzi to search through their files for a decree that would explain the issue. She searches through endless files to no avail. When K. suggests that he does not expect the file to be found, the Chairman says that he can explain the situation without the file. He relates that a few years before, a decree came requesting the service of a surveyor. The Chairman sent a reply back indicating that no surveyor was needed, only the reply went to a different department. Eventually, an influential but distrusting member of the Count's cabinet—an Italian man named Sordini—got involved and sent a memorandum to the Chairman, asking him to defend his reply. Eventually the case was deliberated by Sordini and another official named Brunswick, and they reluctantly concluded that no surveyor was needed.

K. asks why he received a letter from Klamm requesting his services if they were not needed. The Chairman turns to his wife, who is still looking for the decree, and asks her to read the letter from Klamm. She reads it aloud and the Chairman claims that the letter is not official and doesn't state explicitly that he will be taken on as a surveyor. After realizing that his efforts are futile, K. and the assistants leave.

When he arrives back at the inn, the Landlady's husband is waiting outside for him. He leads K. to the Landlady, whose name is revealed as Gardena. She gives him an old photograph of the messenger who had delivered a letter that Klamm had sent her over twenty years ago. Like Frieda, she had once been Klamm's mistress. K. asks how she met her husband, and she explains that after four meetings with Klamm, he never summoned her again. In her sadness, Hans (her husband) consoled her. While they were sitting together, Hans' uncle, the Landlord of the Gentleman's inn whose wife had passed away, offered to lease the inn to Hans and Gardena. They accepted and eventually got married.

K. and the Landlady spend a while talking about Klamm's role in the Landlady's marriage before Gardena asks bluntly why K. insists on trying to speak with Klamm. He replies that he wants to talk to him about Frieda and speak with an official involved with his case. The Landlady gives her consent on the condition that he not try to pursue Klamm himself, but wait for her to try to secure a meeting for him. This is not acceptable to K. who believes that the situation is too urgent, particularly following his distressing meeting with the Chairman. The Landlady says that the Chairman is insignificant and that his wife Mizzi is actually the one in control. Finally the Landlady leaves the lunchroom and K. goes to find Frieda.

When K. arrives at his room, Frieda is talking with the teacher whom K. had met while walking alone on his first day. The teacher tells K. that he was sent on the Chairman's orders. He makes a point to state how kind the Chairman is and how rude K. had been when speaking with him earlier. He says that the Chairman wants to offer K. a position as a janitor at the schoolhouse. The teacher leaves after K. declines the offer. Moments after, Frieda reenters the room. When she finds out that K. has declined the teacher's offer, she gets upset and runs out. She returns with the teacher and explains to K. that the Landlady has decided that K. can no longer stay at the inn. She begs him to accept the position at the school, so they will have a place to stay together, and K. can have temporary employment before things get straightened out at the Castle. K. reluctantly agrees before he gathers his things and heads out to the Gentleman's Inn.

K. arrives at the inn and proceeds to the taproom where he hopes to find Klamm. The bar is dark, so he lights a match and is startled by the shriek of Pepi, Frieda's replacement. K. says that he's searching for Frieda's tablecloth and suggests that she left it in the neighboring room. He says that he would gladly search for it if the room were empty, though he knows that Klamm likes to sit there. Pepi laughs and says that Klamm is not there as his sleigh is waiting for him in the courtyard. K. rushes outside where he hopes to catch Klamm on his way out.

As K. waits in the snow beside the sleigh, he is startled by the voice of the coachman who offers him some cognac. When K. accepts, the coachman directs him into the coach where the bottles are stored in the side pockets. The coach is so warm that K. can not resist lying down for a minute. As he indulges in the cognac, a light comes on and he leaps up in the coach, spilling the cognac on the fur-lined interior. It is not Klamm who arrives from the inn, but another man who asks K. to leave. When he refuses, claiming that he is waiting for Klamm, the gentleman tells the coachman to take the harness off the horses and put the sleigh away. The coachman gives K. an angry look as he follows the orders of the gentleman.

Eventually, the cold forces K. to go back into the inn where he sees Hans, the landlord from the Bridge Inn, who directs him toward the taproom. K. is greeted by Klamm's secretary, Momus, and the Landlady. Momus is meant to engage in an official interrogation of K., but K. refuses to go along with it. Eventually he leaves and heads off toward the school.

As he makes his way in the dark, he comes across his assistants and Barnabas. Barnabas has a letter from Klamm which states how pleased he is with K.'s work and the work of his assistants. Since K. has not done any work yet, he becomes upset at the obvious misunderstanding. K. tells Barnabas to relate the misunderstanding to Klamm and request a personal meeting for him. Barnabas acknowledges K.'s request and agrees to meet him the following day. K. walks the rest of the way to the school with the assistants, content enough with the current situation to let them act as they please.

Soon after they arrive back at the school, K., the assistants and Frieda have dinner. K. whispers to Frieda that they would be better off without the assistants. Frieda eventually agrees and they decide to treat the assistants more harshly. Following dinner, they all try to sleep but it is too cold in the school house. There is a wood shed outside, but it is locked. K. instructs the assistants to find him an axe which he uses to break down the shed door where he and the assistants gather a great pile of wood.

They light a big fire inside the stove and settle down to sleep. There is a noise in the middle of the night that wakes K. He looks beside him and realizes that one of the assistants is curled up next to him where he had expected to find Frieda. K. punches the assistant, causing him to whimper away like a dog. Frieda returns claiming that a cat had sprinted across her face and made the noise that woke K. up. They go back to sleep and wake up the next morning to find Gisa, the schoolmistress, and her students surrounding their bed. The schoolmistress scolds K. for not being up and prepared. In her anger, she knocks their coffee pot off the desk, smashing it to pieces.

K. instructs Frieda and the assistants to get to work, hoping that he can straighten the schoolhouse before the teacher arrives. But before long, the teacher enters with the assistants and starts yelling about the broken shed door. The assistants claim that K. had knocked it down, but Frieda contradicts their claims by saying that she had in fact done it. The teacher turns on the assistants and makes a motion to brandish them for lying, but before he does, Frieda admits that they're telling the truth. The teacher turns his wrath on K. and tries to fire him for his inadmissible actions. K. doubts the teacher's authority to fire him as it was the Council Chairman who hired him. The teacher leaves and says that K. will not remain there much longer.

After the teacher leaves, K. expels the assistants from the room. They leave, but stay outside the door, whimpering and whining to be let back in. Eventually the teacher kicks them outside the schoolhouse. At first, the assistants stand in the snow outside K. and Frieda's window. But when the snow becomes too difficult to manage, they trudge across the grounds and prop themselves up on a fence where they can peer into K. and Frieda's room. Frieda expresses sympathy for the assistants and explains that she believes they are Klamm's emissaries. She says they are infatuated by her, but she would be willing to tolerate them as she believes they may be K.'s best connection to Klamm. K. claims that they mean nothing to Klamm and their actions toward Frieda make K. more determined to keep them away.

Before too long, there is a knock on the door. K. rushes to answer, convinced that it is Barnabas. When he opens the door, he is surprised to find a small boy who introduces himself as Hans Brunswick. He claims that he was disturbed by the schoolmistress' treatment of K. and wanted to help him. He reveals that he and his mother had met K. once before during his respite at Lasemann's house on his first day in town. Hans goes on to admit that his mother is ill and his father is cruel. K. and Hans decide that Hans' parents might be able to help K. in his effort to straighten out the misunderstandings behind his surveying job. They arrange a meeting and then Hans leaves.

Directly after his departure, the teacher flings open the door, admonishes K. and Frieda for not cleaning their space and demands that K. retrieve his lunch. K. agrees to clean and retrieve the teacher's lunch only after the teacher admits that K. has not been dismissed of his duties. When the teacher leaves, Frieda expresses her concern over K.'s sudden willingness to receive orders from the teacher, going on to say that some of his statements during his discussion with Hans reminded her of the warnings which the Landlady had imparted to her. At K.'s urging, Frieda goes on to say that she's beginning to believe the Landlady's assertion that K. is merely using her for her past connection to Klamm and the Castle. She goes on to say how upset she was by K.'s manipulation of the little boy as it was clear that all he wanted was the opportunity to speak with Hans' mother. K. admits that this was indeed his intention, but makes it clear that he is not using Frieda. When K. finally leaves to get the teacher's lunch, he trudges past one of the assistants who starts walking toward the window where Frieda is standing.

The narrative goes on to discuss Schwarzer, the son of the Castle steward who K. met his first night at the Bridge Inn. Schwarzer was apparently in love with Gisa, the schoolmistress, and had taken a position as assistant teacher just to be near her. Though K. reflects on the possibility of seeking his aid, he decides instead to go to Barnabas' house where he can speak with Barnabas' sisters about their brother.

When K. arrives at Barnabas' house, he is greeted by Amalia, the quieter and less congenial sister. She tells him that her brother has not returned yet, and suggests that K. is really there for her sister, Olga. Amalia tells K. that Olga is in love with him and that he is welcome to come over when ever he wants. Finally, Olga arrives and Amalia says that she can give K. the full story about Barnabas as she is his greatest confidante.

K. sits down with Olga and listens as she tells him of Barnabas' plight. She describes the agonizing hours he spends waiting—in an office connected to the Castle—for someone to gaze in his direction. Olga goes on to suggest that one can not even be sure that the Klamm Barnabas is serving is in fact the real Klamm. She describes the futility and helplessness of her brother's situation. K. suggests that it is up to Barnabas to change things, as he is the one with opportunity. Olga concedes that K. has hit on the truth, but says that there is more to it. She speaks of a story regarding Amalia that has tainted the image of her family.

It all took place a little over three years ago at a festival for the fire department. Amalia was a beautiful girl and her father was convinced that she would find a husband at the festival. Though Olga was jealous at first, she too had to concede that Amalia was breathtaking. At the festival, a man named Sortini, who is known as much for his name being close to that of the Castle official Sordini, seemed to be quite enamored by Amalia, going so far as to jump over a little barrier just to stand close to her.

Later that night, after Amalia and Olga had already returned home, a messenger came with a letter for Amalia. Though it was from Sortini, the contents were demanding and repulsive. Amalia shrieked after reading it and tore it to shreds in the face of the messenger. Though she showed a great sense of pride by ripping up the letter, her rejection of a Castle official and her ill treatment of an official messenger became the family's downfall. The entire town, at the subtle urging of the Castle, came to reject them. Their status, which had once been upper middle class, soon plummeted beneath the lowliest peasant.

Initially, K. expresses his outrage at the contents of the letter and support over Amalia's actions. But when Olga begins to draw comparisons between Amalia's situation with Sortini and Frieda's situation with Klamm, K. gets upset and defensive, insisting that there exists no justifiable comparison.

Olga diverts the attention from Frieda and elaborates on the impact Amalia's actions have had on the family. She explains how friends and enemies alike bombarded them with inquiries about the letter, and then systematically turned their backs on them. She speaks of how customers at her father's shoe and leather shop began pulling their orders until he had no customers left. Then a man from the fire department came to the house to take back her father's diploma and make it official that he was no longer a part of the department which he had, only weeks before, been considered a top candidate for deputy chief.

Olga explains that her father sent out an endless series of petitions, to various members of the Castle, asking for a pardon, but since his family wasn't guilty of anything specific, there was no way to receive a pardon. So he decided to try and speak with a Castle official in person. Since he did not have access to the Castle, he took to sitting on a fence by the road that led to the Castle. Everyday, through rain and snow, he sat on that fence, waiting for an opportunity to speak personally with a member of the Castle. After days of sitting in horrid weather, he started experiencing rheumatic pains which eventually became so debilitating that he couldn't leave his bed with out assistance. Now Amalia has devoted her life to their parents' care.

Olga goes on to relate her plan for bringing her family out of the ruins. She claims that if she could explain the situation to Sortini's messenger, he would be able to offer a pardon that would allow the rest of the village to accept the family again. She begins frequenting the Gentleman's Inn with the Castle domestics, inquiring regularly about Sortini's messenger. Though she never finds him, she manages to open an opportunity for Barnabas to seek a position at the Castle. She reveals that the letters he delivered to K. were the first official tasks assigned to him, and that their fate is linked to K.'s.

Soon after nightfall, there is a knock on the door which Amalia answers. When she gets back in the house, she reveals that it was one of K.'s assistants. K. decides to sneak out the back door and return to the school. When he gets to the road, he calls the assistant who claims to have been aware of the back way to the street. The assistant, Jeremias, tells K. that he came to Barnabas' house at the request of Frieda. He informs K. that Artur, the other assistant, has filed an official complaint about him and that Frieda has decided to take back her position in the taproom and stay with Jeremias who has secured a position as a room-waiter at the Gentleman's Inn.

While K. is speaking with Jeremias, they are approached by Barnabas who claims to have had success. Though he never spoke with Klamm, he encounters a man named Erlanger, one of Klamm's first secretaries. Erlanger requested that K. meet him at the Gentleman's Inn where he will be meeting with people until five the next morning. Upon hearing the news, Jeremias darts off toward the Gentleman's Inn, seemingly to get word to Frieda, but K. catches up to him and they walk to the Gentleman's Inn together. When they arrive, K. and Gerstacker, the coachman, are called in together for their meeting with Erlanger. Jeremias is also allowed in as he has secured a position at the Gentleman's Inn. Gerstacker and K. are taken to the hallway outside Erlanger's room. Gerstacker discovers that Erlanger is sleeping and says that they have to wait until he rings for them.

Frieda passes while K. is in the hall, and he stops her long enough to have a conversation. She expresses her feelings of abandonment and betrayal. K. offers his perspective, and adds that he hasn't even eaten. After hearing of K.'s day, Frieda gets him some lunchmeat. Just as they begin to get close again, Jeremias appears from the room that he and Frieda are sharing. He is feverish and wrapped in one of Frieda's shawls. Frieda returns to the room with Jeremias.

K. goes back to the hallway where he had been waiting and finds no one there. He decides to open a random door in hopes of finding Erlanger. After knocking and hearing no answer, he steps inside and is confronted by a voice. K. identifies himself. The man claims to be familiar with K. and introduces himself as Burgel, Friedrich's secretary. He invites K. to sit down on his bed. K. accepts the offer, and Burgel starts to speak about the various trials and rewards of being a secretary. As he speaks, K. grows increasingly weary, finally falling asleep. He is awakened by a knocking and a voice requesting his presence in Erlanger's room. Burgel implores K. to get up, which he finally does.

When he arrives at Erlanger's room, K. finds him dressed to leave in a winter coat and hat. Erlanger expresses his displeasure at having to wait for K. Then he explains that since the members of the Castle are very concerned that nothing disturb Klamm, and they are aware that K. has been living with Frieda, they want him to get Frieda back to work at the taproom before the change becomes burdensome for Klamm. After making his request, Erlanger leaves and K. is left in the corridor where he watches while a servant distributes files from a cart to nearly every room in the hall. After the servant has distributed all the files, a bell starts clanging and K. is ushered off by the landlord. He realizes that the bell was ringing because he was in the hallway without proper permission. K. is brought to the taproom where he sets a board across two barrels and lies down to sleep.

K. wakes up nearly twelve hours later, unsure, at first, whether he had even slept. He is greeted by Pepi who tells him that Gerstacker, the landlady and even Frieda had asked for him and watched him at different points while he slept. Pepi goes on to discuss her promotion and subsequent demotion from the taproom. She tells K. that he was her hero for a few days, as he was responsible for bringing Frieda out of the taproom and making room for her to take her position. But then she explains that Frieda had never really expected to be gone for that long and had manipulated the events of the last few days for her own benefit. She speaks about Frieda's ability to distract those around her from the fact that she's really quite old and ugly. Pepi suggests that Frieda's confident demeanor and invented relationship with a top official allowed her to act as she pleased in the taproom, and even made people, like K., see her as attractive.

Pepi describes her own life as a chambermaid, and how the other chambermaids had made a dress for her when she gained the opportunity to work in the taproom. She suggests that with one more day, Frieda would not have been able to replace her as she would have had sufficient time to show how much more attractive and pleasant she was than Frieda. But Frieda's calculated plan, which included keeping Klamm away from the taproom, wouldn't allow it. According to Pepi, Frieda used K. as a means of regaining some of the respect that had been slipping away from her. Pepi claims that Frieda had made up her mind to run off with the first meager man who came along to show that she was strong enough to give up a prestigious relationship with a top official for a person whom she genuinely loved. However, her plan also included keeping Klamm away from the taproom until she ultimately returned, giving the impression that she was indispensable. All this without regard for Pepi or K., mere tools in Frieda's scheme.

K. counters Pepi's claims by noting her intense imagination and saying that it was little more than his neglect of Frieda that led to her breaking their engagement. He goes on to suggest that the reason Pepi is returning once again to become a chambermaid is that she is not suited to life in the taproom. Pepi says that K. is in love with Frieda only because she left him, but she goes on to ask that he come and live with her and the other chambermaids in the basement of the Gentleman's Inn. She says that he would be well taken care of and he could help them all out. And if he were not happy with the situation, he could leave after the winter.

Their conversation is interrupted by the Landlady who expresses surprise at finding K. still at the Gentleman's Inn. She asks him about a remark he made, before settling down to sleep, about her dress. He says that he doesn't remember, but when the landlady persists with her questions, he admits that he finds her outfit unusual: almost too elegant for her position, and entirely awkward. The Landlady seems both offended and flattered as she reproaches K. for his ignorance while at the same time, asks more of his opinion. She says she'd like to show him the wardrobe closet in her office. Before he is escorted away, Pepi makes arrangements to meet K. at the courtyard door. Soon after the landlady has displayed her collection of clothes, K. steps out of her office and is whisked away by Gerstacker who had been waiting for him. Gerstacker leads him to his cottage and requests that he abandon his position at the school, move in with him and help with the horses. K. suggests that Gerstacker is only helping him because he believes K. can "'get something out of Erlanger.'" Gerstacker admits that this is true and then introduces him to his mother. Kafka's never-completed novel ends—without final punctuation—after K. shakes Gerstacker's mother's hand and strains to hear what she has just begun to say.

LIST OF CHARACTERS IN

The Castle

K. is the primary character in the novel. He is hired as a land surveyor by the Castle, but when he arrives for duty, he finds that certain restrictions prevent him from engaging in his work. Driven by the futile effort to gain access to the Castle, he becomes engaged to the mistress of a Castle official, takes a job as a school janitor and indulges in various conversations and adventures, all of which seem to push him farther away from his ultimate goal.

Frieda works in the taproom and is Klamm's mistress. She eventually leaves her post to become engaged to K., but returns at the end of the novel.

Pepi is Frieda's replacement in the taproom. She loses her post when Frieda returns to work.

Gardena, The Bridge Inn Landlady, is very close to Frieda and tries to protect her from K.

Hans, The Bridge Inn Landlord, is the subservient but lazy husband of Gardena.

The Gentleman's Inn Landlady is a moody woman who insists on showing her wardrobe to K.

Gerstacker is a coachman who gives K. a ride back to the inn in the beginning of the novel. He reappears at the end of the novel and introduces K. to his mother.

Momus is one of Klamm's secretaries.

Barnabas is the brother of Olga and Amalia and a messenger for K.

Olga is Barnabas' sister who tells K. the story of their family.

Amalia is Barnabas' sister who takes care of their parents.

The Assistants (Jeremiah and Artur) work for K. until he relieves them of their duty.

The teacher meets K. in the beginning of the novel and relays the Council Chairman's offer for K. to work as a janitor at the school.

Gisa, The Schoolmistress, is an angry lady who smashes K. and Frieda's coffee pot while they're living at the school.

The Council Chairman speaks with K. and insists that there is no need for a land surveyor.

Mizzi is the Council Chairman's wife.

Klamm is a Castle official to whom K. desperately wants to speak.

Hans Brunswick is a boy whom K. meets at the school.

Burgel is a Castle secretary with whom K. speaks while waiting for a meeting with Erlanger.

Erlanger is one of Klamm's first secretaries.

Schwarzer is the son of a Castle steward who confirms K.'s appointment as land surveyor.

CRITICAL VIEWS ON

The Castle

THOMAS MANN ON KAFKA

[Thomas Mann was a German born novelist who won
the Nobel prize for literature in 1929. His major works
include *The Magic Mountain* and *Doctor Faustus*. In this
excerpt, Mann speaks on the religious element in the
novel.]

For it is plain that regular life in a community, the ceaseless
struggle to become a "native," is simply the technique for
improving K.'s relations with the "Castle," or rather to set up
relations with it: to attain nearer, in other words, to God and to
a state of grace. In the sardonic dream-symbolism of the novel
the village represents life, the soil, the community, healthy
normal existence, and the blessings of human and bourgeois
society. The Castle, on the other hand, represents the divine
dispensation, the state of grace—puzzling, remote,
incomprehensible. And never has the divine, the superhuman,
been observed, experienced, characterized with stranger, more
daring, more comic expedients, with more inexhaustible
psychological riches, both sacrilegious and devout, than in this
story of an incorrigible believer, so needing grace, so wrestling
for it, so passionately and recklessly yearning after it that he even
tries to encompass it by stratagems and wiles.

The question is really an important one, in its own touching,
funny, involved religious way: whether K. has actually been
summoned by the estates authorities to act as surveyor, or
whether he only imagines or pretends to others that such is the
case, in order to get into the community and attain to the state
of grace. It remains throughout the narrative an open question.
In the first chapter there is a telephone conversation with "up
above"; the idea that he has been summoned is summarily
denied, so that he is exposed as a vagabond and swindler; then
comes a correction, whereby his surveyorship, is vaguely

recognized up above—though he himself has the feeling that the confirmation is only the result of "lofty superiority" and of the intention of "taking up the challenge with a smile."

More impressive still is the second telephone conversation in the second chapter; K. himself holds it with the Castle, and with him are his two aides, who possess all the fantastic absurdity of characters in dreams: whom the Castle sent to him, and in whom he sees his "old assistants." And when you have read this, and listened with K. to "the hum of countless children's voices" from the receiver, the rebuff given by the official up above, with the "small defect" in his speech, to the suppliant down below at the inn telephone, with his persistent appeals and tergiversations, you will not lay down this long, circumstantial, incredible book until you have run through and lived through the whole of it; until amid laughter and the discomfort of its dream-atmosphere you have got to the bottom of those existences up there, the heavenly authorities, and their overbearing, arbitrary, puzzling, anomalous, and entirely incomprehensible activities.

—Thomas Mann, "Homage," *The Castle*, by Franz Kafka (New York: Alfred A Knopf, 1954): pp. xiv-xv.

MAX BROD ON *THE CASTLE* AND ITS GENESIS

[Max Brod was Franz Kafka's closest friend and confidant. He has written a great deal about Kafka's life and work, and is largely responsible for bringing his posthumous prose to the public. In this excerpt, Brod speaks on the germ of the novel.]

Translated by Gerhard H. Weiss.

"TEMPTATION in the Village," a twelve-page sketch which Kafka wrote in 1914 (*Diaries*, June 11), contains the germ of *The Castle*. It describes the tragedy of a man who wishes to live in a village with other people but is unable to become rooted in the strange place and to find his way to the Castle which looms forebodingly over the village. The mood of almost hopeless loneliness—and, as regards the villagers, fateful mistrusting and misunderstanding—casts a shadow even in this preliminary sketch; thus, in the very opening a native addresses his wife: "Wait a little. I want to see what that man is going to do. He's a stranger. He's hanging around here for no reason at all. Look at him." Whereupon the hero (of the fragment) replies: "I'm looking for the inn, that's all. Your husband has no right to speak of me that way and perhaps give you a wrong impression of me." Later the wife whispers to another person: "He talks so much." Further criticism of the strange, unwanted intruder is superfluous.

Upon re-reading this suggestive fragment, I was reminded of the connection between Kafka's basic concepts in *The Castle* and a novel by the Czech writer Bozena Nemcova entitled *The Grandmother* (tr. by Francis Gregor; Chicago, 1891)—an affinity not previously noted, to my knowledge.

Bozena Nemcova lived from 1820 to 1862. *The Grandmother*, her main work, an idyllic novel of tender simplicity, was used as a textbook for students of the Czech language in the German secondary schools of Prague. Thus Kafka as a student became acquainted with the wonderfully insinuating and at the same time naive, candid, and wholesome story of the mountain village at the foot of the Riesengebirge. Thus I, too, read it with enthusiasm one year later.

> —Max Brod, "*The Castle*: Its Genesis," *Franz Kafka Today*, eds.: Angel Flores and Homer Swander (Madison, The University of Wisconsin Press, 1958): pp. 161-162.

ALBERT CAMUS ON HOPE AND THE ABSURD IN KAFKA

[Albert Camus was a French novelist, dramatist and philosopher. His major publications include *The Stranger* and *The Plague*. In this excerpt, Camus speaks on the development of the novel.]

Few works are more rigorous in their development than *The Castle*. K. is named land-surveyor to the Castle and he arrives in the village. But from the village to the Castle it is impossible to communicate. For hundreds of pages K. persists in seeking his way, makes every advance, uses trickery and expedients, never gets angry, and with disconcerting good-will tries to assume the duties entrusted to him. Each chapter is a new frustration. And also a new beginning. It is not logic but consistent method. The scope of that insistence constitutes the work's tragic quality. When K. telephones to the Castle, he hears confused, mingled voices, vague laughs, distant invitations. That is enough to feed his hope, like those few signs appearing in summer skies or those evening anticipations which make up our reason for living. Here is found the secret of the melancholy peculiar to Kafka. The same, in truth, that is found in Proust's work or in the landscape of Plotinus: a nostalgia for a lost paradise. "I become very sad," says Olga, "when Barnabas tells me in the morning that he is going to the Castle: that probably futile trip, that probably wasted day, that probably empty hope." "Probably"—on this implication Kafka gambles his entire work. But nothing avails; the quest of the eternal here is meticulous. And those inspired automata, Kafka's characters, provide us with a precise image of what we should be if we were deprived of our distractions[2] and utterly consigned to the humiliations of the divine.

In *The Castle* that surrender to the everyday becomes an ethic. The great hope of K. is to get the Castle to adopt him. Unable to achieve this alone, his whole effort is to deserve this favor by becoming an inhabitant of the village, by losing the status of foreigner that everyone makes him feel. What he wants is an occupation, a home, the life of a healthy, normal man. He can't stand his madness any longer. He wants to be reasonable. He wants to cast off the peculiar curse that makes him a stranger to the village. The episode of Frieda is significant in this regard. If he takes as his mistress this woman who has known one of the Castle's officials, this is because of her past. He derives from her something that transcends him—while being aware of what makes her forever unworthy of the Castle. This makes one think of Kierkegaard's strange love for Regina Olsen. In certain men, the fire of eternity consuming them is great enough for them to burn in it the very heart of those closest to them. The fatal mistake that consists in giving to God what is not God's is likewise the subject of this episode of *The Castle*. But for Kafka it seems that this is not a mistake. It is a doctrine and a "leap." There is nothing that is not God's.

Even more significant is the fact that the land-surveyor breaks with Frieda in order to go toward the Barnabas sisters. For the Barnabas family is the only one in the village that is utterly forsaken by the Castle and by the village itself. Amalia, the elder sister, has rejected the shameful propositions made her by one of the Castle's officials. The immoral curse that followed has forever cast her out from the love of God. Being incapable of losing one's honor for God amounts to making oneself unworthy of His grace. You recognize a theme familiar to existential philosophy: truth contrary to morality. At this point things are far-reaching. For the path pursued by Kafka's hero from Frieda to the Barnabas sisters is the very one that leads from trusting love to the deification of the absurd. Here again Kafka's thought runs parallel to Kierkegaard. It is not surprising that the "Barnabas story" is placed at the end of the book. The land-surveyor's last attempt is to recapture God through what negates him, to recognize him, not according to our categories of goodness and beauty but behind the empty and hideous aspects of his indifference, of his injustice, and of his hatred. That stranger who asks the Castle to adopt him is at the end of his voyage a little more exiled because this time he is unfaithful to himself, forsaking morality, logic, and intellectual truths in order to try to enter, endowed solely with his mad hope, the desert of divine grace.[3]

NOTES

2. In *The Castle* it seems that "distractions" in the Pascalian sense are represented by the assistants who "distract" K. from his anxiety. If Frieda eventually becomes the mistress of one of the assistants, this is because she prefers the stage setting to truth, everyday life to shared anguish.

3. This is obviously true only of the unfinished version of *The Castle* that Kafka left us. But it is doubtful that the writer would have destroyed in the last chapters his novel's unity of tone.

—Albert Camus, "Hope and the Absurd in the Work of Franz *Kafka," Kafka: A Collection of Critical Essays*, ed. by Ronald Gray (Englewood Cliffs: Prentice Hall, Inc., 1962): pp. 151-52.

R.O.C. WINKLER ON KAFKA'S ACHIEVEMENT

[R.O.C. Winkler studied at Cambridge University. His work has appeared in *Scrutiny* and *Kafka: A Collection of Critical Essays*. In this excerpt, Winkler discusses the achievement of the novel.]

The Castle was Kafka's last and greatest achievement in the novel form, and any estimate of his significance as a novelist is bound to start from a consideration of this apotheosis of his method. Here the trends of interest that appear rather diversely in the earlier novels are fused to give an account of the whole range of human experience in what seemed to Kafka its most significant implications. The ultimate concern is religious. In Kafka's view there is a way of life for any individual that is the right one, and which is divinely sanctioned. So much is perhaps admitted by most of our moral novelists; but to Kafka this fact itself constitutes a problem of tremendous difficulty, because he believes the dichotomy between the divine and the human, the religious and the ethical, to be absolute. Thus, though it is imperative for us to attempt to follow the true way, it is impossible for us to succeed in doing so. This is the fundamental dilemma that Kafka believes to lie at the basis of all human effort. He gives some insight into its nature in *Investigations of a Dog*, where the dog-world corresponds roughly to human society and we as humans bear something of the same relationship to the hero as the Castle officials bear to Kafka in *The Castle*. The solution of the Dog's problems is perfectly plain to us, yet we can see that the Dog is constitutionally incapable of ever realizing the solution.

This fundamental problem, however, doesn't present itself to the human mind in naked simplicity. It isn't the Puritan problem of justifying one's behavior in the eyes of God alone. The dilemma is conceived of as becoming known to us only at the ethical level; that is, it emerges as the general problem of the individual's relation to society, and any attempt at a solution must involve an attempt to come to terms with, and find a place in, the social organism. We are told, and it is probably true, that Kafka felt this problem with peculiar acuteness in virtue of his racial isolation as a Jew and his general isolation as a consumptive; but it is important to realize that this only made more keenly felt a difficulty that is implicit in any attempt as social organization, and one that has manifested itself particularly in recent years as a result of the centrifugal tendencies of modern civilization. In "He," *Notes from the Year 1920*, Kafka writes:

> He was once part of a monumental group. Round some elevated figure or other in the center were ranged in carefully thought-out order symbolical images of the military caste, the arts, the sciences, the handicrafts. He was one of those many figures. Now the group is long since dispersed, or at least He has left it and makes his way through life alone. He no longer has even his old vocation, indeed He has forgotten what he once represented. Probably it is this very forgetting that gives rise to a certain melancholy, uncertainty, unrest, a certain longing for vanished ages, darkening the present. And yet this longing is an essential element in human effort, perhaps indeed human effort itself.

One has only to run one's mind over the more significant literature of Kafka's generation, from *St. Mawr* and *The Waste Land* to *Ulysses* and *Manhattan Transfer* to realize how prominent a part this view of modern European civilization has played in determining the artist's attitude to his material. Preoccupation with this problem—the problem presented by the corruption, not of the individual as such, but of the interhuman relationships that give him significance as a member of civilized society—recurs throughout Kafka's work, and is realized most effectively in his short story, *The Hunger-Artist*. Its more positive aspects are persistent throughout *The Castle*, where the hero's whole efforts are directed immediately towards an attempt to establish himself in a home and a job, and to become a member of the village community—to come to terms, in fact, with society.

—R.O.C. Winkler, "The Novels," *Kafka: A Collection of Critical Essays*, ed. by Ronald Gray (Englewood Cliffs: Prentice Hall, Inc., 1962): pp. 46-47.

HEINZ POLITZER ON ATMOSPHERE IN THE NOVEL

[Heinz Politzer was Professor Emeritus at Berkeley before his death in 1978. Remembered as one of the foremost Kafka scholars, he was the author of *Franz Kafka: Parable and Paradox*. In this excerpt, Politzer speaks on the atmosphere of the novel.]

It seems almost certain that Kafka was still occupied with *The Castle* when he described his descent to the underworld to Brod in the letter of July 1922. Indeed, the letter serves as an explicit statement of the atmosphere pervading the novel. The story is populated by ghosts irrationally unleashed by unknown hands. Instead of love it shows the dubiousness of embraces and abounds, quite generally, with specters risen from the underworld of a highly agitated unconscious.

The horror of this ghostly scene is increased by the fact that the Land-Surveyor seems to have sought it out of his own volition. The protagonist has not been "packed off" like Karl Rossmann, nor is he arrested like Joseph K.; he consciously chooses his fate. He goes to the Castle wishing to be acknowledged as the Count's Land-Surveyor. To be sure, he maintains that the Count is expecting him (5),* but having lost his way, he does not know the village into which he has "wandered" and seems unaware of the Castle's existence (4). Long spaces of the novel are devoted to a discussion of the legal merits of K.'s case, but whatever these may be, one fact remains undisputed: K. was not forced to appear here. If he was called, he was also free to disregard the call. Yet he responded to whatever real or imaginary voice he heard. Thus K.'s attitude is immediately distinguished from the attitudes of Kafka's other central figures by a greater degree of independence. He decides to enter the Castle, and when he finds it impossible or too difficult to achieve this aim, he concentrates on bringing about a personal interview with Klamm, the Court Official in charge of Land-Surveyors. As much as any man is free to exert his will, K. thinks, speaks, and acts in freedom. Even when he has almost exhausted his energies, he can say, "I came here of my own accord, and of my own accord I have settled down in this place" (258).

In this respect he resembles the man from the country, who, like him, has come to the Law of his own accord but will never leave it voluntarily. At least in their complete inaccessibility the Law of the parable and the master of the Castle are closely related, and we shall not be surprised to meet the image of the door in all its ambiguity as often here as we did in *The Trial*. The line of doorkeepers reappears in the bureaucracy of the Castle, from the village elders up to Klamm. Their corruption flavored with understanding is the same; of the officials in the Castle it is also said that they "accept bribes simply to avoid trouble and discussion, but nothing is ever achieved in this way" (276). And it is more than probable that the final words of the doorkeeper in the parable are just as valid for the more aggressive Land-Surveyor K. as they are for the passively stubborn bank employee Joseph K.

NOTE

*Numbers without letters refer to the American edition of *The Castle* (1954).

—Heinz Politzer, "*Der Verschollene:* The Innocence of Karl Rossmann," *Franz Kafka: Parable and Paradox*, (Ithaca: Cornell University Press, 1962): pp. 220-21.

JAMES ROLLESTON ON CHARACTER

[James Rolleston has been a member of the Department of German at Yale University. He is the author of *Rilke in Transition: An Exploration of his Earliest Poetry*. In this excerpt, Rolleston discusses the characters in the novel.]

A technique used by Kafka to suggest the "provisional" quality in his protagonist is presentation from the outside. The paradoxical combination of the hero's perspective with such momentary withdrawals, found already in "Description of a Struggle," occurs frequently in the first chapter of *The Castle*: "K. did not change his position, did not even once turn round, seemed quite indifferent, and stared into space." Compelled to view K. from the outside, the reader feels the strengths, as well as the exposure, of the outsider's posture. K.'s uninvolved assessment of Schwarzer's telephone manner and the Castle's workings shows his absorption in strategy to be formidable equipment for an outsider's identity. When the Castle, in momentary disarray, appears to solidify this identity by rejecting K., his response is cool to the point of abstraction: "To escape at least the first shock of their assault he crawled right underneath the blanket." The Castle then recovers and puts itself into a position to convert K.'s strategic strength into weakness by confirming his appointment.

The next paragraph ("K. pricked up his ears..."), crucial to an interpretation of K., is full of ironies that suggest K.'s future dependence on the Castle at the moment of his most vivid declaration of independence. He is obviously right to see the appointment as a form of challenge, but because he cannot see the strength of his present position he fatally misstates the relationship. The Castle does indeed know "everything necessary about him (alles Nötige über ihn)," namely, that he is a potential transformer of the system who must be fended off at all costs; its initiation of the struggle is thus hardly "with a smile" (*lächelnd*). K. perceives his appointment, correctly, as an effort by the Castle to coopt him and blunt his effort to achieve an identity through a direct relationship. But in this it turns out that the Castle has made a just (rather than an under-) estimation of him. For, like the man from the country in "Before the Law," K. has an inadequate idea of the meaning of freedom. He feels that freedom can be quantified, equated with intellectual lack of attachment, and then applied in larger or smaller doses as the relationship with the system seems to require. He does not see that one is either inside or outside the system, with no compromise possible. He fails to realize that, at the moment when he begins to reckon out the amount of freedom he can expect, he has in fact forfeited the only valid freedom, the freedom to relate to the Castle without any regard for its preferred modalities.

K. awakes the next morning determined to confront the Castle, making strategic use of the advantage he feels his appointment has given him. But gradually he becomes involved with village life, symbolized by the universal snow making everything more "definite" and more uniform. Given the intricacies of each individual snow crystal, there is no paradox in observing that the world of the village is both alive in every detail and undifferentiated in its overall patterning. On one level K. is one of the "forms" being gently covered by the Castle's snow: none of the four meetings with village inhabitants that take place during the remainder of this chapter is really initiated by K. He allows the landlord to satisfy an apparent urge to talk to him; while contemplating the Castle K. is "disturbed" (*gestört*) by the schoolteacher's presence; when the exhausted K. throws a snowball against the nearest window, the response—"the door opened immediately (Gleich öffnete sich die Tür)"—is as if he were expected; and Gerstäcker, who appears to know K.'s identity in advance, addresses him without prompting. However, it would be wrong to conclude, as too rigid an application of Walser's theory would seem to indicate, that the Castle is moving monolithically to counter K.'s self-assertions. In the villagers of the Castle we see fully developed what the narrator of "The Great Wall of China" has hinted at in his compatriots: fundamental oneness with the system and impenetrably sceptical individualism. "Total ambivalence," earlier the property of the hero-narrator, has been transferred to the environment, automatically invalidating K.'s efforts to establish his function, despite illusions of progress. For it is a feature of the reopened structure Kafka has developed here that the two basic currents— K.'s abstract relationship with the Castle and his human ties to the village—by no means coincide, and as a rule move in opposite directions. To take two obvious examples: at the moment of K.'s greatest success, the winning of Frieda, he experiences a sense of total alienation that rightly foreshadows how far this relationship will take him away from the Castle in its abstract form; and, of course, the moment of total human defeat and exhaustion is also the moment of proximity to success in Bürgel's room. Between these extremes every encounter of K.'s entails the possibility of movement on both levels. And while I incline to agree with Walser that "development" would contradict the basic conception of K.'s "character," Kafka has infused the novel's structure with so strong a feeling of the possibility of development that several critics, most notably Gray and Emrich, detect an actual change in K. towards the end of the existing text.

—James Rolleston, "Reopened Structure: *The Castle*," *Kafka's Narrative Theater*, (University Park: The Pennsylvania State University Press, 1974): pp. 119-21.

MARTHE ROBERT ON THE ASSISTANTS

[Marthe Robert has been considered France's most prominent Kafka scholar. She has translated many of his works and has written several critical studies including *Origins of the Novel* and *As Lonely As Franz Kafka*. In this excerpt, Robert speaks on K.'s treatment of the assistants.]

At the beginning of the novel, K., who claims to have been summoned to the Village as a surveyor, announces the imminent arrival of his assistants and of the instruments with which they have been entrusted. A little later he meets "two young men of medium height, both very slim, in tight-fitting clothes," who amaze him with their resemblance to each other and the extraordinary speed with which they move through deep snow. Himself struggling desperately to get ahead, he wants very much to attach himself to them, in other words, make use of them as assistants, but no sooner has he called out to them than he loses sight of them completely. On entering the inn, he sees the same young men stationed on either side of the door, obviously waiting for him. "'Who are you?' he asked, looking from one to the other. 'Your assistants,' they answered. 'It's your assistants,' the landlord corroborated in a low voice. 'What?' said K., 'are you my old assistants, whom I told to follow me and whom I am expecting?'" Thus K. does not know his own employees; or, more exactly, he does not recognize them, though in some obscure corner of his mind he knows that these young men belong to him and have long been in his service ("my old assistants"). This, of course, is absurd; in broad daylight, or even in the half-light where this story takes place, there can be no rational explanation for such a mixture of knowing and not knowing unless we assume that K. is insane or deliberately lying; and yet, as we go deeper into his relations with his two strange acolytes, we are forced to recognize that this apparently irreducible absurdity constitutes in itself the logic of the novel.

K. treats the assistants who have come to help him with his hypothetical surveying (they have not brought their instruments, and, of course, they know nothing whatever of this kind of work) with a brutality that seems quite inexplicable when we consider how he lets them invade his privacy. True, the young men are no better than Blumfeld's assistants; despite their exaggeratedly manly beards, they are infinitely childish, docile and timid, lazy, untruthful, and lecherous, yet (like the two characters in caftans in Lateiner's *Meshumed*, who had so struck Kafka's imagination years before), disarming in their innocence and awkwardness. But though in his relations with them K. conducts himself like a ruthless master, conscious of his rights and of his superiority, he is quite incapable of defending himself against their constant meddling in his most intimate affairs. For in reality their mission has nothing to do with the surveying K. talks so much about; their mission is simply to be with him at all times of the day and night, and from this task their master, who has become their slave, is powerless to deflect them.

—Marthe Robert, "Fiction and Reality," *As Lonely As Franz Kafka*, (New York: Harcourt Brace Jovanich, Publishers, 1979): pp. 185-186.

[Charles Bernheimer has been a professor of English and Comparative Literature at the State University of New York. In this excerpt, Bernheimer speaks on the allegorical elements within the novel's protagonist]

As a compulsive misreader and obsessive lover of *Geschwätz*, K. in *The Castle* is an allegorical protagonist precisely insofar as he strives for, and thereby postpones, knowledge. He is a land-surveyor in the sense that his vocation is to delimit differences, to map out boundaries, in order to establish the symbolic principle relating possession to authority, ownership to its origin, material presence to an absent but recuperable presence. His ambition is to be a successful reader of the symbolic structure binding Castle and village, and he feels that his very existence depends on this success. For him, as for many critics of Kafka's texts, symbolic interpretation ensures the meaningful unity of life, its comprehensibility within a totalizing system of signification. K. is a cypher searching for a name, a beginning sign questing for a nominal conclusion. That such a conclusion never comes indicates that, in the fallen world, no sign can be any more than a partial signifier. The questing interpreter, K. or his belated critic, is forever frustrated by an allegorical structure that fragments, temporalizes, and textualizes his symbolic search.

The bridge K. traverses in the opening paragraph of the novel involves a "going-over" similar to the psychopoetic crossing I analyzed in the parable "On Parables." K. crosses not into a settled world of fixed meanings (the abode of traditional allegorical translations) but into a shifting, unstable world out of which no exit is possible for him. The "illusory emptiness" (p. 481; p. 3) his searching gaze seeks to penetrate from the bridge suggests, through its ambiguous reference to either a momentarily absent presence or the permanent void of an illusion, the kind of duplicitous play of signification that will henceforth determine K.'s existence in a state of suspension, as an exile on the *pavlatche* (to use the image I elaborated in the previous chapter). This play deconstructs one of Western culture's central images of hierarchic and differential order: the powerful castle dominating a subservient village at its feet. K., surveyor of differences, assumes that the function of this order is to define the sacred and the profane, the good and the evil, a principle of inclusion and exclusion, standards for legality and transgression, the existential terms of significant freedom and random absurdity. But from the outset the crucial difference between Castle and village is subverted, and with it the very possibility of a stable and coherent symbolic *Verbindung* such as K. seeks to establish.

The subversion of this Erotic enterprise is subtly initiated already in the first speech of the novel when Schwarzer informs K. that "this village is the property [*Besitz*] of the Castle and whoever lives here or passes the night here does so, in a certain measure [*gewissermassen*], in the Castle" (p. 481; p. 4). This statement defining the Castle–village relationship in terms of *Besitz* can be elucidated by the aphorism I have already quoted about the limitations of language: "For all things outside the phenomenal world, language can be employed only in the manner of an allusion [*andeutungsweise*] but never even approximately in the manner of a comparison [*vergleichsweise*] since in accordance with the phenomenal world it is concerned only with property [*Besitz*] and its relations" (H, p. 45; DF, p. 40). The Castle is like language in its concern with property relations and its limitation to the phenomenal world. Any reading of the Castle in symbolic terms, binding village and Castle in a *Vergleich*, would violate the allusive quality of that "certain measure" that keeps them apart even as it breaks down their differences. Yet K.'s vocation of *Landvermesser* almost seems to have been called forth to perform just this violation, to make the *Masse* (measures) *gewiss* (certain) through "a series of destructions." Indeed, K.'s need for precise measurement appears to arise in reaction to his initial questioning response to Schwarzer's statement: "Into what village have I strayed [*mich verirrt*]? Is there a Castle here?" (p. 481; p. 4). This village is the space of K.'s *Verirrung*, a space defined by the radical undecidability of the Castle's existence.

—Charles Bernheimer, "The Allegorical Structure of *The Castle*," *Flaubert and Kafka: Studies in Psychopoetic Structure*, (New Haven: Yale University Press, 1982): pp. 198-199.

IRVING HOWE ON *THE CASTLE*

[Irving Howe was Distinguished Professor Emeritus at the Graduate Center of the City of New York and co-editor of *Dissent* magazine. His publications include *The American Newness* and *World of our Fathers*. In this excerpt, Howe speaks on the themes at the heart of the novel.]

At the very heart of *The Castle* (Ch. 15) there is a long interspersed narrative which I take to be essential to an understanding of this novel—and here I diverge from most of the familiar Kafka interpretations.

A young woman named Olga, modest and thoughtful, tells K. the story of her accursed family: how the other villagers shun the Barnabas family as a nest of pariahs because her sister Amalia had rejected the sexual advance of a Castle official; how her brother keeps tormenting himself with questions as to whether he really is a messenger employed by the Castle ('he goes into the offices, but are the offices part of the real Castle?'—and for that matter, what if there is no 'real Castle?'); how her aged father keeps begging for a 'pardon' from the Castle officials on behalf of his daughter Amalia, begging even for a moment's notice, which they blandly or haughtily refuse.

Amalia, the younger sister of Olga, had been singled out by Sortini, a Castle official, who sent her a vulgar note proposing that she immediately come to bed with him. Nor is this an exceptional demand: other Castle officials have also ordered village girls to serve as mistresses. Amalia, however, tears Sortini's letter into bits. For this act of defiance, the family suffers ostracism, not directly from the Castle officials but from the pliant villagers.

What are we to make of this? One Kafka commentator has

described Amalia's behaviour as 'the pride of those who will not serve' the gods; evidently mortals must obey. The Italian critic Pietro Citati, in his recent book on Kafka, writes that 'we must not draw the mediocre conclusion [from the Amalia–Sortini episode] that the divine is simply a deceit', though he fails to explain why, if there is deceit, it should be regarded as divine or if it is divine, it should not be subject to moral judgment. We must not, writes Citati, submit this incident to 'the test of reality', though what other test mortal readers can bring to bear I do not know.

I cite Citati because his views are not uncommon, and behind them lies an assumption that piety entails abasement and faith, unquestioning obedience. Nowhere in Kafka's text, however, is this assumption supported; nowhere is it suggested that the Castle, simply because it is the seat of authority, merits absolute submission or should not be put to 'the test of reality', which is to say, the test of our judgment. Some Kafka critics, intent upon accepting the ways of the Castle as a transcendent value, fall back upon the justifying comparison between Amalia's ordeal and God's command that Abraham sacrifice Isaac, which is said to be another instance of the Kierkegaardian notion of a 'teleological suspension of the ethical'. Leave aside whether Abraham's readiness to sacrifice his son is quite the marvel of faith it is often taken to be, and leave aside, as well, the question of whether we can or should suspend 'the ethical'. Let us simply recall that in the Biblical story an angel does appear in order to save Isaac and that God does not insist upon the ultimate test of bloodshed— while under the reign of Kafka's Castle there is no reason to expect a similar intervention. Had Amalia gone to Sortini, as other village girls have gone to Klamm, he would not, we may suppose, have renounced the pleasure of taking her.*

NOTE

*The Yiddish poet H. Leivick recalls that upon hearing as a schoolboy the story of Abraham and Isaac, he asked his teacher, 'But what if the angel had been late?' This little boy was evidently incapable of a 'suspension of the ethical'.

—Irving Howe, "Introduction," *The Castle*, by Franz Kafka (New York: Alfred A. Knopf, 1992): pp. xvi-xvii.

PLOT SUMMARY OF

The Trial

The Trial, one of Franz Kafka's three posthumously published novels, opens in Frau Grubach's boarding house where Joseph K., the principal character, wakes to the knocking of two warders, Franz and Willem, who give him notice of his arrest. When Joseph asks for an explanation of the charges, they claim to know only that he is under arrest, and not the charges against him. Joseph wonders whether he is the subject of some joke, played on him in honor of his thirtieth birthday. He discounts this theory when he thinks of how many people would have to be involved. Finally he gets called to a room, normally inhabited by Fraulein Burstner, to meet with the Inspector. When he arrives, there are three other men ruffling through pictures in the corner. He realizes that these men are not warders but Rabensteiner, Kullich and Kaminer, fellow employees of the bank where he works. Much to Joseph's displeasure, the Inspector is not able to tell him about his case, only that he is under arrest, and that he will not be prevented from going to work and engaging in his normal activities.

Joseph leaves with his three colleagues, and they catch a taxi to the bank. The day progresses normally, Joseph receiving some kind acknowledgements regarding his birthday. Though he returns home late, he makes a point to speak with Frau Grubach who assures him that she does not believe the unique arrest that took place earlier in the morning was anything to worry about. Joseph inquires about Fraulein Burstner—in whose room his meeting with the Inspector took place—and Frau Grubach tells him that she is at the theater and will likely return home late. Joseph goes back to his room and decides to wait up for her.

When Fraulein Burstner returns, Joseph whispers through a crack in his door that he would like to speak with her before she goes to sleep. Reluctantly, she invites him in and he explains that he is to blame for a meeting that took place in her room. Joseph asks for permission to move her furniture around so he can demonstrate how the proceedings occurred. Though Fraulein Burstner is not excited by the prospect of letting Joseph move her furniture around, she ultimately consents. As he's acting out the role of the Inspector, he yells rather loudly and wakes the Captain who is a guest of Frau Grubach. Fraulein Burstner implores Joseph to leave, but before he does, he kisses her face and neck with surprising voraciousness.

The following day, while at work, Joseph receives a phone call informing him that his first interrogation will take place on Sunday at the Court of Inquiry. Upon hanging up the phone, he is greeted by the Assistant Manager who invites him to a party that same Sunday. Joseph replies that he is already committed that day. The Assistant Manager then proceeds to make a phone call, and despite the length of his conversation, Joseph remains standing beside the phone until the conversation ends. He admits that he was never told the specific time that he was meant to arrive at his appointment. The Assistant Manager suggests that he call back, but Joseph claims that it is not important enough to do that. He silently decides that he will arrive at nine o'clock, as that is when the courts usually open.

Joseph wakes up late on Sunday morning. He takes a taxi to the address, but realizes that he was never told where in the building the interrogation was meant to take place. He decides that it wouldn't be appropriate for him to ask the children and other residents who are around the location of the Court of Inquiry, so he knocks on as many doors as he can and says he is looking for a joiner named Lanz. As he is ready to give up the search, he knocks on one last door and is swept inside. Though he continues to suggest that he's looking for Lanz, he is led into a packed room where he is spoken to almost immediately by the Examining Magistrate who says that he is an hour and five minutes late.

Following a brief pause, the Examining Magistrate asks Joseph to confirm that he works as a house painter. Joseph, who is actually a chief clerk at a bank, rebuffs the Magistrate's claim, causing the assembly to applaud on his behalf. Joseph uses the error and the brief applause as an opportunity to indulge the assembly with a tirade about the proceedings. He describes how he was treated by the warders and how their aim seemed to be to tarnish his reputation. He goes on to insult the warders, the

Inspector and the Examining Magistrate. He concludes by suggesting that the proceedings are meaningless and that even simple-minded people like his landlady, Frau Grubach, could recognize their pettiness. It is at this point that Joseph realizes that the members of the assembly are all wearing the same shield as the Examining Magistrate. He feels betrayed and decides to leave the court. He is met at the door by the Examining Magistrate who informs him that he has lost any advantage that an interrogation may have provided him. Joseph leaves in disgust.

Despite the claim that he would not return to the Court, Joseph comes back the following Sunday at precisely the same time. When he arrives, a woman outside the courtroom tells him that there is no interrogation scheduled for that day. The woman is standing next to some sizable books about which Joseph inquires. The woman responds by saying that she would not be allowed to show him what is inside as they are the Examining Magistrates books. The woman goes on to apologize for causing a disturbance in the courtroom the previous week. She says that the student whom she embraced is infatuated with her and that his affections have become so common that even her husband has accepted them.

As the conversation continues, Joseph makes mild advances toward the woman. With his hand over hers, she offers to help with his case. Joseph asks again to see the Magistrates books and this time she concedes. What he finds seems irrelevant to his case, and he makes an irritable claim that the employees of the court are lazy and ignorant. The woman counters by suggesting that the Magistrate works very hard and often quite late. She says that following Joseph's case, he was up nearly all night writing in his books. She goes on to add that she brought him a light by which to write, and he returned it that evening and paid her a generous compliment. She reveals that he even sent her a pair of stockings as additional thanks, implying that he too holds a certain infatuation with her.

When Joseph starts to make bolder advances, he is disrupted by a law student named Bertold who asks to speak with the woman in the neighboring room. Before long, Bertold and the woman are embracing. Joseph pounds his fist in fury until he is confronted by the student who suggests that he leave. When Joseph says that it is the student who should leave, Bertold lifts the woman in his arms and carries her up the stairs. Joseph follows for a few steps before the woman tells him that he is carrying her to the Examining Magistrate.

While Joseph is reflecting on the unusual circumstances, the woman's husband, who works as an usher for the court, returns. Joseph tells him that the student carried his wife up to the Examining Magistrate. The woman's husband says that there is nothing he can do. He tells Joseph more about this unfortunate situation and then offers to take him upstairs where the court offices are located.

There are a number of people lining the hallway upstairs, and the usher explains to Joseph that they are all defendants like himself. Joseph asks the nearest defendant what crime he is accused of. At first, the man seems incapable of answering, but he is finally able to relate that he has filed affidavits regarding his case and he is waiting for some kind of feedback. Joseph tells him that he has done nothing and could not imagine wasting so much time and energy on his own case. Then he asks the man if he believes that Joseph has been arrested. When the man doesn't answer, Joseph shakes him by his collar and throws him against the wall.

When the usher is finally able to lead him away, Joseph starts to feel anxious and confined. He asks the usher to show him the way out, but the usher says that he first needs to deliver his letter. Though Joseph gets upset, he finds himself too weak to do anything about it. He is approached by a man and a woman who recognize that he is feeling ill. The woman remarks that it is not uncommon for people to feel faint in the law offices as they are very stuffy and hot. The man, who turns out to be the Clerk of Inquiries, determines that Joseph should be escorted outside. Joseph makes it clear that this is indeed what he wants. When it is clear that Joseph can stand it no longer, the man and the woman escort him down the stairs and outside where the cool breeze brings him back to health.

Joseph spends the next few days trying unsuccessfully to speak with Fraulein Burstner. He rearranges his schedule and sends letters to her office and her residence trying to set up a meeting. When Sunday rolls around and Frau Grubach, who had been taking special care of Joseph since their mild dispute over Fraulein Burstner, delivers his breakfast, he inquires about the noise that is filling the hallway. Frau Grubach explains that a French teacher named Fraulein Montag is moving in with Fraulein Burstner. As the conversation proceeds, a maid knocks on the door and tells Joseph that Fraulein Montag would like to speak with him in the dining room. He accepts her invitation.

After grabbing a coat from his closet, Joseph walks to the dining room to meet Fraulein Montag. She explains that Fraulein Burstner asked her to speak with him and explain that she has not been feeling well and doesn't believe that a meeting is necessary. After Fraulein Montag delivers her message, Frau Grubach's nephew, Captain Lanz, walks into the dining room and makes a grand display of kissing Fraulein Montag's hand. Joseph decides to slip away, but instead of going back to his room, he knocks on Fraulein Burstner's door. After receiving no answer, he enters her room. He notices that everything looks vastly different than when he was last there. When he leaves the room, he realizes that Fraulein Montag and the Captain could see him, so he walks hastily to his room.

Mid-way through the next week, Joseph is preparing to leave his office when he hears a noise coming from the lumber room. He walks to the door and stands beside it. He hears sighing sounds from inside, and opens the door to find the warders, Willem and Franz, beside another man brandishing a whip. Willem and Franz explain that they are being whipped because Joseph had complained about them. Joseph says that he merely stated what had happened on the day of his arrest. Willem and Franz plead to Joseph to try and stop the whipping. Though he tries to persuade the whipper not to inflict punishment, the man refuses. Joseph decides to leave the room, closing the door to prevent an approaching clerk from taking notice. The next day, Joseph opens the lumber room, and to his surprise, he finds the same three still there. He slams the door at once and asks a subordinate clerk to clean the lumber room as soon as he can.

A few days later, while Joseph is at work, his uncle Karl shows up and asks to speak with him. Joseph's uncle admits that his daughter Erna, who also lives in the city, had written him a letter, explaining that she had come to visit Joseph at the bank, but had not been able to see him because he was talking to an official about his trial. Joseph admits that what his cousin has written is true. Uncle Karl is upset by this news and asks Joseph to provide him with details. Since Joseph is worried that fellow employees might be listening, he suggests that they take a walk. Once they're outside, Uncle Karl tries to convince his nephew to move out to the country with him, but Joseph says that he wouldn't want to appear as if he's fleeing the scene. Uncle Karl hails a cab and he and Joseph head off to the home of a man named Huld who is a lawyer and an old school mate of Joseph's uncle.

When they arrive at the lawyer's house, they knock on the door and a young woman tells them that Huld is sick and that he's not taking any visitors. Joseph's uncle makes it clear that he's an old friend and he should be allowed in. He bangs on the door out of frustration until the woman reveals that the door is open. When they get inside, the woman leads them by candlelight to Huld's room. Joseph is very attracted to the woman whose name is Leni. When they get to the room, Uncle Karl greets his old friend who is lying in bed. He sits down and asks Leni, the maid, to leave, but she refuses. Huld supports her by saying that she is entitled to hear anything they might discuss. But when Huld realizes that his friend has not come for a sick visit, but to get counsel on his nephew's trial, he dismisses Leni and grows increasingly animated.

Huld is aware of Joseph's case and claims that it is too intriguing for him to pass up, despite his health. Joseph is surprised that Huld knows of his case, but Huld explains that he has many visitors from the court. Then he reveals that the Chief Clerk of the Court is sitting in the room as they speak. Both Joseph and his uncle are surprised to discover that there is indeed another man sitting in the dark shadows of Huld's room. Soon after the clerk joins the discussion, there is a loud crash in the hallway. Joseph offers to investigate the noise and leaves the room.

When Joseph steps into the hallway, he is pulled into a room by Leni who claims that she threw a plate against the wall in order to lure him out. They express their mutual affection for one another. Leni says that she can help Joseph, but he would need to plead guilty first. Then she asks him if he's involved with anyone, and Joseph shows her a picture of Elsa, a woman with whom he spends time occasionally. Leni coaxes him to admit that she's not that important to him and declares that Joseph is hers. Joseph sees a painting on the wall of a person who seems to be a high judge. Leni reveals that it is merely an Examining Magistrate who had himself painted in such a way out of vanity. Finally Joseph leaves and steps into the street. His uncle is waiting outside in the rain. He pushes Joseph against the door and berates him for abandoning the lawyer and the Chief Clerk and jeopardizing his case for the sake of a maid whom he believes is Huld's mistress.

Following a few draining weeks which Joseph spends consumed by his case, he finds himself in his office at the bank, devoid of energy. He wonders if any progress has been made, and considers dismissing Huld. He knows that he has been working on the first plea for weeks now and has yet to submit it to the court. He toys with the idea of writing the plea himself. Before he can come to a conclusion, he agrees to see the manufacturer who had been waiting all morning to see him.

The manufacturer comes in holding a large file of documents and immediately starts talking of his proposal for a business transaction that has great possibilities. Though Joseph is able to follow along at first, he quickly loses focus and just goes through the act of attention until the manufacturer finishes talking. While Joseph pretends to review the documents, the Assistant Manager comes in to his office and the manufacturer springs from his seat, eager to share his proposal with Joseph's colleague. Joseph is relieved when the manufacturer follows the Assistant Manager to his office.

As soon as Joseph is alone again, his thoughts return to his case. He considers again whether to let his lawyer go. While he grapples with this decision, he is disrupted by the manufacturer's return. To Joseph's surprise, the manufacturer reveals that he is aware of Joseph's case. He says that there is a painter named

Titorelli who supports his artistic ambitions by making portraits for the Court. The manufacturer encourages Joseph to visit Titorelli as he has surprising influence over the Court officials. The manufacturer writes a note for Joseph to bring to Titorelli's home and then he leaves.

Joseph decides to set out immediately for the painter's home, but as he's leaving the bank, he is confronted by three gentlemen who have been waiting hours to speak with him. Joseph does his best to brush them off, until the Assistant Manager appears again and offers to help the gentlemen for Joseph. Though he is not happy about the idea that the Assistant Manager is moving in on his clients, Joseph feels he has no choice but to accept his colleague's help. Before he leaves, he walks back into his office and finds the Assistant Manager rummaging through his papers. He says he is looking for a particular document which he suddenly claims to have found. He takes a sizable folder off Joseph's desk and returns to his own office. Joseph is not happy about having his files and personal space violated, but he feels helpless to the needs of his case and sets out for the painter's home.

Titorelli lives in a decrepit building in a poor part of town. Joseph makes his way into the building and is confronted by a hunch-backed girl and a number of other girls. Joseph asks where the painter lives. The hunch-backed girl runs up the stairs, never bothering to respond. Joseph follows her past a group of girls who are huddled together, watching with eager eyes. The hunchbacked girl leads Joseph to Titorelli's door, and he is greeted by the painter who twirls the girl around and sets her back on the floor. He introduces himself to Joseph and admits that the girls have not left him alone since he painted one of their portraits.

Joseph hands Titorelli the letter written by the manufacturer. The painter reads the letter and throws it on his bed. He shows Joseph one of the portraits he's working on. He explains that the Court officials are vain and are permitted to get portraits that suggest loftier positions than their actual ones. Finally, the painter brings up Joseph's case and asks if he is innocent. Though Joseph claims he is, the painter makes it clear that the Court assumes guilt, and it is only through behind-the-scenes manipulating that this assumption can be changed. He goes on to explain that he inherited his position as Court painter from his father and that there is no one else who can do what he does. This distinction makes him particularly valuable, and gives him the power to be influential. Then he explains that there are three ways that Joseph can spare himself: "definite acquittal, ostensible acquittal, and indefinite postponement."

Titorelli claims that his influence, though significant, can only guarantee an ostensible acquittal or an indefinite postponement, and he asks Joseph to decide which one he'd prefer. Titorelli explains that an ostensible acquittal could not guarantee an absolute acquittal, as his influence is with the lower judges and the ultimate decision comes from the higher officials. He also explains that an acquittal of this sort could not guarantee that he wouldn't be arrested again. The indefinite postponement, on the other hand, would make it unlikely that he would be arrested again, though it would take a great deal of energy to keep his case from being actively addressed and his overall freedom would be somewhat restricted. The painter says that both methods "'prevent the accused from coming up for sentence,'" to which Joseph counters, demonstrating his understanding, "'but they also prevent an actual acquittal.'"

After Titorelli is certain that Joseph has grasped the essentials, Joseph puts his coat back on and makes it clear that he has to leave. The painter then pulls a few paintings of landscapes out from beneath his bed and asks Joseph if he'd be interested in buying one. Realizing that he had never discussed any compensation for the painter's services, he agrees to buy every painting Titorelli pulls out, despite that they all seem to depict the same scene. As Joseph is leaving through the back door beside the painter's bed, he realizes that there are Court offices next door. The painter explains that the offices are in many attics around the city. Joseph takes a cab back to the bank and has the paintings brought into his office.

After ample reflection, Joseph decides that he's going to dismiss his lawyer. So in the late evening, he takes a taxi over to Huld's residence and knocks on the door. Following a lengthy pause, the door is opened by a small old man named Block. Joseph asks if he lives there, and Block replies that he's just one of Huld's clients. Joseph asks if he's having an affair with Leni. Block seems surprised by the question and assures Joseph that he is not. Finally Joseph follows Block into the kitchen where Leni is fixing soup for Huld. His first question to Leni is whether she is having an affair with Block. She refers to Block as a "miserable creature" and asks him to confirm again that they are not having an affair. Then Leni asks Joseph if he'd like her to announce his presence to Huld. After some deliberating, Joseph decides to allow Leni's boss to eat first.

When Leni leaves to deliver Huld's soup, Block, who identifies himself as a tradesman, starts talking about his court case. He tells Joseph that he has given up his practice to devote himself entirely to his case. He admits that he has gained little valuable information throughout the five years that his case has been going on, and confides that he has hired other lawyers in addition to Huld. He claims that Huld has a tendency to stretch the truth, suggesting that his lawyer's propensity to refer to himself as one of the great lawyers is an exaggeration at best, as he is clearly a small case lawyer. Though Joseph finds Block's perspective to be interesting and valuable, he begins to worry about the whereabouts of Leni.

When Leni returns, Block ceases his conversation. Leni explains to Joseph that Block often sleeps in the maid's chambers, desperate for any opportunity to speak with Huld. As Joseph starts to make his way toward the lawyer's room, Block reminds him that he had promised to divulge some information. Joseph responds by saying that he is going to dismiss Huld. Block repeats Joseph's words with childish excitement. Leni runs after Joseph who makes his way into the lawyer's room. Though Leni tries to prevent him from closing the door, he is eventually able to force her arm away and shut her out.

The lawyer greets Joseph and asks him to take a seat. He says that he has a few things to talk to him about, and that he will not see him at such a late hour in the future. Joseph responds by saying that the lawyer's request is fine with him, and goes on to say that he plans to dismiss him of his services. The lawyer is rather surprised, but asks Joseph to give him the opportunity to persuade him otherwise. He goes on to say how little Joseph understands about the nature of such cases and that what he fails to realize is how well he has been treated. After listening to the lawyer's statements, Joseph makes it clear that he still intends to dismiss him. Huld asks for one last chance to convince Joseph otherwise, and proceeds to ring for Leni whom he asks to get Block.

Block enters the room cautiously and approaches Huld's bed as if it were a shrine. The lawyer ignores him at first, but finally turns toward the tradesman and admonishes him for not being timely. He goes on to mention that he spoke with a judge earlier in the day about his case, but refuses to say what they spoke about. When Block gets on his knees before the lawyer, Joseph remarks on his pathetic behavior. Block responds harshly toward Joseph, suggesting that he's no better. Finally Leni coaxes the lawyer into telling Block about the conversation he had with the judge. Huld says that the judge suggested that Huld was wasting his time with Block, and that his case had not even begun. Block is shocked by the news, but when he starts to get restless, he is scolded again by the lawyer. He eventually settles down and resumes his humble, subservient demeanor. Although it is clear that Joseph is turned off by the lawyer's actions, the reader is left to assume that he will dismiss him of his services, as the chapter is never completed and the matter is not addressed again.

The narrative continues a few days later when Joseph is at the bank, waiting to take a high profile Italian client to tour the Cathedral and other local sights. Though Joseph does not feel comfortable with the time he has been spending outside the bank, he feels that he is not in a position to refuse such a responsibility. Joseph, who had arrived early in an effort to organize things in his office, is called almost instantly into the Manager's office to greet the Italian client who had arrived earlier than expected.

When he makes it to the Manager's office, Joseph greets the client in rehearsed Italian and waits as he speaks to the Manager in a speedy dialect which Joseph can not follow. Toward the end of their conversation, the Manager, aware that Joseph was not able to understand everything, explains that the client has an appointment that will not allow him to tour the entire city, but will allow for an extensive tour of one place. Therefore, Joseph is to meet him at the Cathedral at ten o'clock.

Joseph is happy for the opportunity to spend a few more hours in his office, though he makes sure to arrive punctually at ten. It is raining when he arrives at the Cathedral. After looking around the outer grounds, he decides to wait inside. The Cathedral is empty, and the poor lighting makes it difficult to see. Just when Joseph believes that the Cathedral is empty, a priest emerges and ascends to the pulpit. Joseph decides to leave before the priest begins his sermon, as he doesn't want to get forced into staying longer than he has to. As he starts to leave, the priest addresses him by name and reveals that he is aware that Joseph is on trial. He acknowledges that the case is not going well for Joseph and suggests that Joseph lessen his dependency on other people, women in particular. Joseph defends the potential effectiveness of employing a woman's assistance, but agrees that things have not gone as smoothly as he would have hoped.

Joseph wonders why the priest insists on standing behind his pulpit, and asks him to speak to him face to face. The priest finally descends to Joseph's level and tells him a story of a man who wished to gain access to the law, but was denied by a doorkeeper. According to the priest, the doorkeeper told the man that he could not grant access, but if he chose to wait, it was not inconceivable that he could be granted access. Though the door was open, the man decided against a forced entry and agreed to wait to be properly admitted. The man waited a lifetime, but received no invitation. Before he died, the man asked the doorkeeper why no one else ever attempted to gain access to the law through this open door, and the doorkeeper explained that the door was solely for him, and that the time had finally come for the door to be closed.

Joseph and the priest discuss the details of the story, each offering their respective interpretations. Finally, Joseph says that he has to leave, and the priest, identified as the prison chaplain, shows him out.

The final chapter takes place at nine o'clock, the night before

Joseph's thirty-first birthday. Two men dressed in long coats and top hats arrive at his room and escort him out to the street. Upon seeing a policeman, they run with Joseph to the edge of town, stopping at a field beside a quarry. The men remove Joseph's shirt and lay him down on a rock. They take out a butcher's knife and pass it back and forth, as if deciding who should be the one to use it. A man leans his head out of the window of a nearby house. As Joseph tries to identify the figure in the window, one of the long-coated men grabs his throat while the other drives the knife into his heart.

LIST OF CHARACTERS IN

The Trial

Joseph K. is the primary character of the novel. He is arrested in his room at Frau Grubach's boarding house, but the charges are never explained. He spends the novel growing increasingly consumed by the cryptic details of his case. In the process of preparing for a potential trial, his performance at the bank begins to decline. He hires and fires a lawyer, befriends the Court painter and interacts with a variety of people, none of whom help relieve his budding anxiety. At the end of the novel, he is led away by two men who eventually kill him.

Frau Grubach owns the boarding house where Joseph stays and is ultimately arrested.

Willem and Franz are the warders who arrest Joseph in the boarding house.

Rabensteiner, Kullich and Kaminer are employees at the bank. They are present at Joseph's meeting with the Inspector.

Fraulein Burstner lives in the boarding house where Joseph is arrested.

Montag is a French teacher and Fraulein Burstner's friend.

The Captain (Lanz) is Frau Grubach's nephew.

The Assistant Manager works at the bank with Joseph. He seems to capitalize on Joseph's dwindling performance.

Uncle Karl helps Joseph find a lawyer.

Dr. Huld is the lawyer who Joseph's uncle helps him find. Joseph eventually relieves him of his duties.

Leni works for Huld. She and Joseph have a brief romantic encounter.

Block, the Tradesman, is one of Huld's clients.

The manufacturer tells Joseph about Titorelli.

Titorelli, the Painter, makes portraits of Court officials. He offers to help Joseph.

The Examining Magistrate leads Joseph's first and only interrogation at the Court.

Bertold is the law student who works with the Examining Magistrate.

The Priest speaks with Joseph at the Cathedral.

CRITICAL VIEWS ON

The Trial

RENE DAUVIN ON MEANING IN *THE TRIAL*

[Rene Dauvin was a scholar and an essayist whose work
has appeared in such literary volumes as *Franz Kafka
Today*. In this excerpt, Dauvin addresses the many
interpretations of the novel.]

Translated by Martin Nozick.

The Trial is so mysterious, so vague, that many interpretations are
possible. As we stand on the threshold of Kafka's work, we feel
uneasy, disoriented. The very form and structure of the novel
amaze us, for it escapes all classification and transports us into an
atmosphere of hallucination and strange disquiet. There seems
to be no apparent continuity in this world. Did Kafka, then,
abandon himself to the meanderings of dreams? I do not think
so. We must take Joseph K. to be the alter ego of Kafka. The
author of *The Trial* and his hero are both obsessed by strange
visions which haunt their sleep. How can one rid himself of these
anguished specters that inhabit the most diverse layers of the
subconscious and which are ready to rise to the surface the
instant awareness of reality flags? Psychoanalysis tells us that this
can be done by an effort of the consciousness which brings the
specters out into the light. And that is precisely what Kafka does.
Literary composition was for him a sort of catharsis. That is why
The Trial is a plunge into the night, a long nightmare which takes
us through the stifling atmosphere of the darkest regions of
Kafka's ego.

    Joseph K. is arrested one morning after getting up. This is the
hour, according to Kafka's *Diary*, when "healthy men disperse the
phantoms of the night." But with him, "the phantoms return as
the night wears on, and in the morning they are all there, only
they are not recognizable." Thus, K.'s arrest is the beginning of
a nightmare or, more exactly, of a series of nightmares. The

action, therefore, takes place in Kafka's soul, and the plot is symbolic of manifest or repressed tendencies. The characters of *The Trial*, whether they argue with K. or agree with him, are aspects of his ego. The novel is a dialogue Kafka has with himself; it is not by chance that one of the police-inspectors actually bears the name "Franz." In his dreams, Kafka becomes aware of the deep antagonisms which tear his being apart. But he is not the master of his nocturnal visions. He allows himself to be guided by them, a fact that explains the alogical composition of the novel. These nightmares haunt him at night and on Sundays—in other words, during those hours when the congeries of daily toil no longer spreads a projective screen of banal tasks over the subconscious. That is why Joseph K. is summoned to court either at night or on Sundays. Furthermore, Joseph K., more aware than Kafka's other characters, knows very well that this mishap could not have happened to him at the office. "In the Bank, for instance, I am always prepared," said Joseph K., "nothing of that kind could possibly happen to me there. I have my own attendant, the general telephone and the office telephone stand before me on my desk, people keep coming in to see me, clients and clerks, and above all, my mind is always on my work and so kept on the alert." What, then, are these long, stifling corridors leading nowhere, these ghostlike judges with their phantom beards, these dark attics, if not the nocturnal universe of Kafka or Joseph K.? Now we know the climate in which the novel unfolds. The dream-key is the one that opens the door to this world. Let us now search out the keys which will provide the interpretation of the novel and will disclose to what extent the problems of life inspired Kafka.

—Rene Dauvin, "*The Trial*: Its Meaning," *Franz Kafka Today*, eds. Angel Flores and Homer Swander (Madison: University of Wisconsin Press, 1958): pp. 145-146.

HEINZ POLITZER ON *THE TRIAL* AGAINST THE COURT

[Heinz Politzer was Professor Emeritus at Berkeley before his death in 1978. Remembered as one of the foremost Kafka scholars, he was the author of *Franz Kafka: Parable and Paradox*. In this excerpt, Politzer discuss the proceedings within the novel.]

As the title indicates, *The Trial* is not focused on the fate of the bank clerk Joseph K. but on the proceedings to which he is subjected. These proceedings are Kafka's theme, and Joseph K. can claim to play the role of the protagonist only because the Trial needs him to become manifest. He is a *Mann ohne Eigenschaften* (in Robert Musil's phrase), a nondescript man, devoid of spectacular deficiencies and virtues. His personal tragicomedy stems from the fact that he, in his mediocrity, is called upon to respond to demands that even a character of impressive stature would find impossible to fulfill. Above all, Kafka does not seem to be interested in the psychological development of his hero during the year of the trial (as, on the level of the apprenticeship novel, he still had been in *Der Verschollene*). As a human character Joseph K. shows as little body and soul as the monolinear figures Kafka drew on the margins of his manuscripts. K. is a literary image, and not a portrait, let alone the self-portrait of his author.

Since the novel is told from K.'s human point of view, it is bound to give the impression that its action consists of K.'s idle attempts to discover his guilt. This, however, would lower *The Trial* to the level of a mystery story in which the crime has to be ferreted out, not the criminal. It also would reduce the Trial itself to a mirror "of the process which starts in any man who is suddenly forced to master and justify his life in its totality."

It is the reality of the invisible Court of Justice that permeates the story with its presence, and K. is nothing but the visible object chosen by the Court to prove its claim to adjudge man. The Court's effort to prove K.'s guilt to him are at least as fruitless as K.'s own attempts to discover his crime. Not only does the man try to penetrate into the interior of the Court, the Court also does its best to reach the conscience of K., to present the case made against him as justified and to induce him to atone actively.* Yet K. and the Court miss each other. Both movements, K.'s quest and the Court's pursuit, run past one another and lead to nothing. The metaphysical world of the Trial and the everyday sphere of K. have lost their common meeting ground.

In his "Reflections" Kafka once coined a very enlightening simile for the state of affairs, as he perceived it in *The Trial*: "The crows maintain that a single crow could destroy the heavens. There is no doubt of this, but it proves nothing against the heavens, for heavens simply mean: the impossibility of crows" (*DF*, 37). The tangible creature, the crow, and the absolute which it has become impossible for the creature to grasp, the heavens, appear as mutually exclusive. If the heavens (Kafka's plural serves to remove them still further from the realm of reality) desire to take possession of the crow, they have to materialize; that is, they must stop being heavens. From the first page of the novel to the last, from the corrupt warders who arrest K. to the grotesque gentlemen who execute him, the Court has to send emissaries who seem to deride the principles both of law and of its sanctity. Even the Chaplain who emerges from the mystical darkness of the Cathedral shows "truly Satanic" traits. Law has to renounce its very essence, justice, in order to confront man, just as the heavens would have to give up their very nature and take shape if ever they intended to meet a crow. Another of the "Reflections" reads: "A cage went in search of a bird" (*DF*, 36). This aphorism includes the parabolical content of *The Trial*. In its desire to communicate with man the Court of Justice has to choose messengers and use a language which must appear to K. as hostile as a cage seems to a bird. The surrealistic absurdity of this cage image contains in a nutshell the paradox underlying the novel. And yet, in the final analysis, there is a great amount of truth in this simile. Just as it is highly improbable that the search of a cage for a bird could ever be successful, so little does the Court of Justice, seemingly equipped with infinite power and a like store of information, succeed in convincing K. of his guilt. It wins the Trial only by slaughtering an ultimately unconvicted victim.

NOTE

*If K. is exposed to the trial, then the Court is likewise exposed to the grasp of K. This double exposure distorts the picture.

—Heinz Politzer, "*The Trial* against the Court," *Franz Kafka: Parable and Paradox* (Ithaca: Cornell University Press, 1962): pp. 166-67.

RONALD GRAY ON HUMOR IN THE NOVEL

[Ronald Gray has been an editor, a critic and literary essayist. His publications include *Goethe the Alchemist, Kafka's Castle*, and *Brecht*. In this excerpt, Gray speaks on the humor in the novel.]

Kafka's humor is less often mentioned, and of course it is not present in all his works, although even the most gruesome often have a touch of it. People find affinities with Mack Sennett comedies, Disney cartoons, music-hall clowns, and Charlie Chaplin, and one recalls Max Brod's account of Kafka's friends bursting into laughter as he read *The Trial* aloud. No one has presented this "grave and casuistical" humor more tactfully or with more evident appreciation than Edwin Muir, who found the root of it in the realization of the complete incompatibility of the ways of Providence and the ways of man. Yet in the very assertion of this incompatibility, which many agree to be the fundamental perception of Kafka's work, there appears to be a contradiction of the "unity of meaning" to which Beissner refers. On the one hand, there is this identity of all layers of meaning, the concrete detail with its "constant sense of apocalyptic significance"; on the other there is this reiterated assertion of utter remoteness, of the impossibility of communicating—there is Kafka's injunction to his friend to burn his manuscripts and never to republish anything that had already appeared in print. There is the achievement we see, and the utter rejection of it. Perhaps this is the genuine paradox, that the moment of defeat, as Muir has it, is the moment of victory, and that the moderately stated tragedy is the most immoderate in its effect, to paraphrase Camus. Nevertheless, it is not unjust to ask whether only such extremes as Kafka embodies in his life and in his work are truly liberating. Joseph K. dies "like a dog"; K. never knows of his liberation, however much he may change in the course of the novel; the officer of the penal colony dies untransfigured, with the iron spike piercing his forehead; Gregor Samsa is swept away with the rubbish, Georg Bendemann drops from the bridge into the river. Is this not a reflection of what Erich Heller calls the identification of life with Evil, a Gnostic loathing of physical reality which will rest content with nothing short of total self-annihilation? To lose one's life to save it, that is a paradox at least verbally familiar to us. But if there is meant to be any "victory in defeat" in these stories, the defeat seems to consist in a quite unallegorical extinction. Gregor Samsa is swept away and that is that; there can be no "sterilization" of that fact. Are we not rightly impelled, in the face of it, to make such a protest as Edmund Wilson's, denying that such "meaching compliance" can possibly be the mark of either a great artist or a moral guide? The ways of Providence may be different from the ways of men, but if they are "so different that we may as well give up hope of ever identifying the one with the other," suicide or indifference are the only alternatives. Erich Heller rightly recalls to us the perverse pleasure which Kafka felt at the "turning of a knife" in his heart. And surely the thoughts of Joseph K. near the end of *The Trial* are revoltingly unacceptable, when he realizes that his executioners expect him to finish the job for them and seems to suppose that only such compliance will satisfy the supreme authority: "He could not completely rise to the occasion, he could not relieve the officials of all their tasks; the responsibility for this last failure of his lay with him who had not left him the remnant of strength necessary for the deed." What else could be implied by this, but that the giver of life and strength requires self-destruction from men, and cruelly withholds the power to achieve it? K. does not fail to kill himself because he prefers to live; he merely resents the vindictiveness of an authority which demands suicide and yet renders it impossible. A more gruesomely untragic ending can hardly be imagined.

—Ronald Gray, "Introduction," *Franz: A Collection of Essays*, ed. Ronald Gray (Englewood Cliffs: Prentice-Hall, Inc., 1962): pp. 3-4.

[Michel Carrouges has been a prominent French critic and essayist. His publications include *Kafka versus Kafka*. In this excerpt, Carrouges compares the themes of the novel with Kafka's story "The Penal Colony."]

In *The Trial* one finds the dark pyramid of involved trials that Kafka instigated in secret: First, the trial of the son, Joseph K., by the father, hidden behind the labyrinthian processes of justice, for the son's crime is that of not having had the strength to love his fiancée to the point of accepting marriage; and only the father, not ordinary justice, could take it upon himself to reproach the son for it. Next, the same trial turns against the father, for it is the overwhelming image of the father that saps the strength of the son and deprives him of the courage to marry. This is doubly manifest in the miserable familial setting of the courtroom in *The Trial* and in the way in which the son flouts the father's power manifested in the job that he imposes on the son (the bank, the image of the insurance office) and behind the tyranny of justice (the image of the familial, social, and religious demands inculcated by the father). Finally, it is also the trial of the son by the son, since Franz delights in emphasizing the gratuitous provocations of Joseph K., his useless acts of rebellion, and ultimately his willing acceptance of condemnation and death.

In *The Penal Colony*, the two themes of suicide at the father's command (*The Judgment*) and legal execution (*The Trial*) are fused into a single act of sacrificial suicide through voluntary substitution for a condemned man on the torture machine. This is the most terrifying myth that Kafka created. Here one finds the traits of the father in the former commandant and those of the son in the person of the officer-victim. But it is not only a myth of terror, for the torture machine evokes directly the sexual process as the black and mechanical process of self-destruction, the myth of the "bachelor machine" in which all Kafka's suffering and anguish find their culmination.* There can be no more tragic illustration of his famous aphorism:

Celibacy and suicide are on similar levels of understanding, suicide and a martyr's death not so by any means, perhaps marriage and a martyr's death (*DF*, 77).

The relationship that he introduces then between celibacy and suicide, marriage and martyrdom, is the equation of facts for which he could find no solution. Between celibacy and marriage he did not cease to wander along a perpetually oscillating trajectory of unstable love affairs.

Therein lies the principal factor behind his tragic odyssey of love. For in spite of what he had said in the letter to his father about the shame of marriage, in spite of the vacillations in his sexual and love life, he admired marriage as the highest of possible human realities:

Marrying, founding a family, accepting all the children that come, supporting them in this insecure world and even guiding them a little as well, is, I am convinced, the utmost a human being can succeed in doing at all (*DF*, 183).

Further on he insists once again:

Marriage is certainly the pledge of the most acute form of self-liberation and independence. I should have a family, the highest thing that one can achieve, in my opinion, and so too the highest thing you have achieved; I should be your equal ... (*DF*, 190).

NOTES

*It is impossible here to go into the long analysis that I devoted to this aspect of Kafka's life and work in the special study entitled *Les Machines célibataires* (The Bachelor Machines), based on a detailed confrontation between Kafka's network of symbols and that of Marcel Duchamp's famous *Large Glass* (*La Mariée mise à nue par ses célibataires*). While waiting to take advantage, in a new edition of my study, of several interesting remarks contained in M. Mayoux's article (*Bizarre*, Nos. I and II), I should like to express my deepest thanks to those who were kind enough to encourage me in its undertaking, particularly Marcel Duchamp, whose personal letters at the time brought me expressions of the highest esteem I could ever have hoped for.

[M. Carrouge's study, *Les Machines célibataires* (Paris: Arcanes, 1954), is now out of print but is currently being translated into English for publication in Great Britain by the house of Jonathan Cape. For a detailed discussion of Duchamp's *Large Glass* and its symbolic implications, which includes several brief references to M. Carrouge's 1954 study, see: Robert Ledel, *Marcel Duchamp* (New York: Grove Press, 1959), pp. 30–33; 70–73 (trans. note).]

> —Michel Carrouges, "The Elusive Bride," *Kafka versus Kafka*, (University of Alabama Press, 1962): pp. 41-43.

James Rolleston on Identity

[James Rolleston has been a member of the Department of German at Yale University. He is the author of *Rilke in Transition: An Exploration of his Earliest Poetry*. In this excerpt, Rolleston speaks on the novel's movement toward the rejection of identity.]

The plunge at the end of *The Trial* from reaffirmation to rejection of an adopted identity is embryonically present at the beginning in K.'s oscillation, partly experimental, partly involuntary, between acceptance and rejection of his arrest (the involuntary element stemming, as we have seen, from the Court's blocking of all the mental exits). When K. first emerges from his room we are told that he moved "as if wrenching himself away from the two men (machte eine Bewegung, als reisse er sich von den zwei Männern los)"; but when told of his arrest he is neither surprised nor hostile, but neutrally inquiring: "So it seems ... But what for? (Es sieht so aus ... Und warum denn?)" The arrest is, in this minimal sense, welcomed as a hard fact upon which he must base his role; and the minimal commitment to the arrest becomes sufficient to undermine all opposing self-assertions. This scene is then replayed a few minutes later when K. reemerges from his room, armed with his papers and having made the crucial decision to "play along" (*mitspielen*). The papers formalize his ambivalent posture, their verbal order laying the foundation of the public identity Josef K. is seeking to establish: producing them is an implicit acknowledgment of the Court's legitimacy as well as a defiant act. Gone is the relative simplicity of "But what for?" This time, when told that he is arrested, K. responds: "But how can I be under arrest: And particularly in such a fashion? (Wie kann ich denn verhaftet sein? Und gar auf diese Weise?)" The "manner" of his arrest is thus both the evidence for its factuality and the proof of its impossibility. Similarly, the simple gesture of revulsion from the warders is transmuted into a complex combination of verbal aggression with an aloof, tactical involvement: "'[The law] probably exists nowhere but in your own head,' said K.; he wanted in some way to enter into the thoughts of the warders..." That this tactical aggressiveness reflects an inability to respond "directly" has already been made clear: "Without wishing it K. found himself decoyed into an exchange of speaking looks with Franz, none the less he tapped his papers..." Having never functioned without the props of convention, K. cannot now do so; he has no "self" that could exist independently of the Court. This explains why K. persists with his "identity" despite repeated failures, and why he seems so little concerned with "self-preservation": when he opts, in Titorelli's room, for total acquittal, he is following the least "safe" course because he is impelled by the dynamics of his identity, which insists on simultaneous involvement and independence, accepting the Court's jurisdiction while rejecting its claim to limit his freedom.

Oscillation between acceptance and rejection, verbal experimentation and gestural repetition: these are the rhythms underlying K.'s effort to project an autonomous role in this first chapter. But his attempt to write his own script is doomed because all initiative is in the hands of the Court; whenever he builds up momentum, he finds that the Court seems to be monitoring his thoughts as well as his actions, always withholding from him the "overview" (*Überblick*) without which he cannot master the situation. Walter Benjamin, stressing that in Kafka's world "man is on the stage from the very beginning," points out that "whenever figures in the novels have anything to say to K., no matter how important or surprising it may be, they do so casually and with the implication that he must really have known it all along." Whereas Gregor Samsa has to contend only with the strictly logical consequences of the transformation, Josef K. finds that all his responses, however "normal," are reduced to schematic fragments of the Court's preordained script. All his words and gestures instantly become suspended in an analytic vacuum, subject to review by himself, by the Court, and by the reader. Gregor's one asset, continuity of context, is denied to Josef K.

—James Rolleston, "Closed Structure: *The Trial*," *Kafka's Narrative Theater*, (University Park: The Pennsylvania State University Press, 1974): pp. 76-77.

WALTER H. SOKEL ON THE NOVEL AND "THE DREAM"

[Walter H. Sokel has been a prominent voice in literary criticism. His publications include *Franz Kafka: Tragik und Ironie* and *Franz Kafka*. In this excerpt, Sokel speaks about the parallels between the novel and "The Dream."]

The parallels between Josef K.'s execution in *The Trial* and his death in "A Dream" are very strong. In both cases an inner "duty" seems to compel K. to his death. In K.'s waking life, it is the Court, through its executioners, that brings this "inner law" to K.'s consciousness; in his dream, it is an artist. In the novel, he realizes "that it would have been his duty to seize the knife, as it traveled from hand to hand above him, and plunge it into himself" (*P*, 271). In "A Dream," two men, who correspond to the two executioners in the novel, hold a gravestone in the air and as soon as K. appears, thrust it into the ground so perfectly that it stands "as if cemented there" (*PC*, 171). But from behind the executioners a third man emerges "whom K. immediately recognized as an artist." At once the artist sets to work inscribing on the gravestone with "golden letters" issuing "from an ordinary pencil ... HERE LIES." But something impedes him;

he cannot continue his work; "he let the pencil sink and ... turned towards K." K. feels miserable. The artist's frustration grieves him; he cries and sobs into his hands. The artist tries to go on with his work, but the former luster of the golden letters fades and is gone. With great effort, he manages to write a capital J—Josef K.'s first initial—but then loses his patience and stamps on the grave mound. "At long last K. understood him" (PC, 172). With his bare hands, he rapidly digs his own grave and sinks into it. While K. is

> received by the impenetrable depths, his name on high was racing with mighty flourishes across the stone.
> Enchanted by this view he woke up (SE, 147).

In K.'s dream the artist assumes the role of the Court in making K. aware of his destiny. In both death is seen as a duty, a personal law which both times K. seeks to obey. In both works, K. while alive is felt to be an obstacle to someone else's progress. In "A Dream" this is transparent. In *The Trial* it is expressed with extreme indirection and subtlety. When on his second Sunday in the Court, K. forays into the attic where the offices of the Court are located, he feels sickened by the close air. "The girl" who is a member of the Court bureaucracy points out to him that he cannot stay because he would "disturb the intercourse (or traffic)" and "K. asked with his glances what intercourse (or traffic)" he was disturbing (P, 86). The German word used by Kafka in this passage is "Verkehr" which can mean both "traffic" and "intercourse," and thus includes not only the spatial and commercial, but also the sexual aspect of interaction among human beings. We find here an obvious echo of the concluding words of "The Judgment"—the "unending *Verkehr*" which coincides with and outlasts Georg Bendemann's self-removal from life. His death brings back infinite life to the bridge that had seemed lifeless when he had been alive. We are likewise reminded of Gregor Samsa's self-removal from his family which, as the last scene of the story makes abundantly clear, is only now enabled to re-enter that stream of procreative life which Gregor's existence had seemed to dam up and inhibit. The "severely" beautiful girl of the Court is coupled with a male figure, the

Court usher who had let K. into the Court offices. The pair confronts him, "looking at him" in such a way "as if in the next minute some great metamorphosis would have to happen to him which they did not want to miss" (*P*, 85). The standard English translation uses the word "transformation" (*T*, 83), instead of "metamorphosis" for the German word "Verwandlung" which has both meanings. Thereby it obscures Kafka's important verbal reference to his earlier work "Die Verwandlung" (The Metamorphosis) which only consistent employment of the same English equivalent for Kafka's term is able to convey. In addition to the allusion in the term "metamorphosis," a subtle connection between Gregor Samsa's fate and the Court offices of *The Trial* is established.

—Walter H. Sokel, "The Three Endings of Josef K. and the Role of Art in *The Trial*," *The Kafka Debate: New Perspectives For Our Time*, ed. Angel Flores (New York: Gordian Press, 1977): pp. 335-36.

WINFRIED KUDSZUS ON THE NOVEL'S ENDING

[Winfried Kudszus has been a prominent German critic and essayist. He is the author of "Erzahlhaltung und Zeitverschiebung in Kafkas Prozess und Schloss." In this excerpt, Kudszus speaks about how the novel ends in despair.]

Similar tendencies are present in *The Trial*. We recall that the development of perspective in this earlier work parallels that of *The Castle*. However, *The Trial* does not emphasize the possibly positive, future significance of an essentially senseless world. *The Trial* ends in despair.

Nevertheless, even *The Trial* does not present the dissolution of perspective and individuality in an utterly gloomy light. At the beginning of its final chapter though, this dissolution appears in a most negative way:

While still on the stairs the two of them tried to take K. by the arms, and he said: "Wait till we are in the street, I'm not an invalid." But just outside the street door they fastened on him in a fashion he had never before experienced. They kept their shoulders close behind his and instead of crooking their elbows, wound their arms round his at full length, holding his hands in a methodical, practised, irresistible grip. K. walked rigidly between them, the three of them were interlocked in a unity which would have brought all three down together had one of them been knocked over. It was a unity such as can hardly be formed except by lifeless matter. (*T*, 280–281)

A little later, K. is repelled by the "cleanliness of their faces" and, at the same time, he sees "the gentlemen" as *one*:

"Perhaps they are tenors," he thought, studying *their* heavy double *chin*. He was repelled by the ... cleanliness of their faces. One could literally see that the cleansing had been at work in the corners of their eyes, rubbing *their* upper *lip*, scrubbing out the furrows at the *chin*. (*T*, 281; italics mine)

In the further development of the final chapter, K.'s repulsion changes into joyful consent. K. now separates himself from his individuality and experiences the "joyous" sensation of total agreement with the world:

"The only thing I can do now," he told himself, and the correspondence between his steps and the steps of the other two confirmed his thought, "the only thing for me to go on doing is to keep my intelligence calm and analytical to the end. I always wanted to snatch at the world with twenty hands, and not for a very laudable motive either. That was wrong...." (*T*, 282)

It was wrong that Joseph K. tried to take his life into his own hands and "stubbornly" resisted the "inevitable" machinery of the world. Now K. is finally "initiated": "In complete harmony all three now made their way across a bridge in the moonlight..." (*T*, 282–283).

Just before K.'s death, the recognition of extra-individual elements, the departure from personal intentions and perspectives, appears weakened. K., the individual, does not want to submit entirely to ultimate and unknown powers:

K. now perceived clearly that he was supposed to seize the knife himself, as it traveled from hand to hand above him, and plunge it into his own breast. But he did not do so, he merely turned his head, which was still free to move, and gazed around him. He could not completely rise to the occasion.... (*T, 285*)

Immediately afterwards, however, K. once more turns away from individuality and perspective. And this time not because of violent pressure, but a vision of salvation which, if only for a moment, extends far beyond individual perspectives: "His glance fell on the top story of the house adjoining the quarry. As a light flares up, the casements of a window there flew open; a human figure ... leaned abruptly forward and stretched both arms still farther. Who was it? A friend? A good man? Someone who sympathized? Someone who wanted to help? Was it one person only? *Was it everybody?* Was help at hand?" (*T*, 285–286; italics mine).

> —Winfried Kudszus, "Changing Perspectives in *The Trial* and *The Castle*," *The Kafka Debate: New Perspectives For Our Time*, ed. Angel Flores (New York: Gordian Press, 1977): pp. 389-91.

HENRY SUSSMAN ON INTERPRETATIONS OF *THE TRIAL*

[Henry Sussman has been director of comparative literature at the State University of New York at Buffalo. His published works include *Afterimages of Modernity* and *High Resolution: Critical Theory and the Problem of Literacy*. In this excerpt, Sussman relates the many interpretations of the parable within the novel to the interpretations of the novel itself.]

Just as the Parable of the Doorkeeper provides for an open-ended—virtually infinite—range of differing and at times mutually contradictory interpretations of itself, so too has *The Trial* sustained interpretations from every significant critical school or attitude of twentieth-century thought. In this surely consists its primary importance, its receptivity to commentary, its solicitation of the different frameworks and attitudes making up intellectual experience. Joseph K.'s circumstances and experiences are interesting from psychological, sociological, and political points of view. Kafka utilized his legal training on the staffs of worker's compensation insurance companies in Prague. As Klaus Wagenbach has stated, he was one of the few "bourgeois" writers of the century to incorporate the misery and suffering he encountered through his professional work into his fiction. A rich literature of Marxist interpretation has arisen in response to the novel. The irrationality and unpredictability of Court operations, the immediate pretext for the Parable of the Doorkeeper, bear striking similarities to Sigmund Freud's descriptions of the unconscious in *The Interpretation of Dreams* (1900) and other works contemporaneous to Kafka's life and writing. *The Trial*, while belonging to the body of fantastic literature, is quite realistic from the perspective of twentieth-century psychological understanding. Its psychological verisimilitude surely constitutes a major element of its readerly appeal.

Kafka's choice of a legal setting for his novel endows it with a procedural or methodological dimension. *The Trial* is simultaneously both a paradigmatic work of fiction and a working example of the theories of literature and its criticism. It has sustained important interpretations from New Critical, structuralist, and deconstructionist points of view. A feminist exploration into the nature and implications of the sexual and power of relationships has begun. *The Trial* is by the same token a fascinating artifact to all schools of philosophy and theology concerned with issues of exegesis and hermeneutics.

For purposes of the present introduction to the critical reception of *The Trial*, I should like to divide the scholarship into its general literary, psychoanalytical, sociopolitical, theological, theoretical, and biographical segments. Bearing in mind the needs of English-language readers, I will emphasize, without intending to slight others, contributions either written in English or available in translation. I have incorporated full bibliographical references into the text of this overview. I am indebted to Richard Jayne, a most creative scholar at Göttingen, whose death in 1991 constituted a serious loss to Kafka studies, for pointing me to some of the more recent additions to the critical literature.

—Henry Sussman, "The Trial of Interpretation and Its Critical Reception," *The Trial: Kafka's Unholy Trinity*, by Henry Sussman (New York: Twayne Publishers, 1993): pp. 21-22.

WORKS BY

Franz Kafka

The Stoker: A Fragment, 1913.

Meditations, 1913.

Metamorphosis, 1915.

The Judgment, 1916.

In the Penal Colony, 1919.

A Country Doctor, 1919.

The Hunger Artist, 1924.

The Trial, 1925.

The Castle, 1926.

Amerika, 1927.

The Great Wall of China and Other Pieces, 1933.

Parables in German and English, 1947.

The Penal Colony: Stories and Short Pieces, 1948.

The Diaries of Franz Kafka, 1948-49.

Selected Short Stories, 1952.

Parables and Paradoxes, in German and English, 1958.

Metamorphosis and Other Stories, 1961.

Short Stories, 1963.

The Complete Stories, 1971.

Shorter Works, 1973.

I Am A Memory Come Alive: Autobiographical Writings, 1974.

WORKS ABOUT
Franz Kafka

Adorno, Theodor. "Notes on Franz Kafka." *Prisms*, trans. Samuel and Shierry Weber. London, 1967.

Atler, Robert. *Necessary Angels: Kafka, Benjamin, Scholem.* Cambridge: Harvard University Press, 1990.

Anderson, Mark, ed. *Reading Kafka.* New York, 1989.

———. *Kafka's Clothes: Ornament and Aestheticism in the Habsburg "Fin de Siecle."* Oxford: Oxford University Press, 1992.

Beck, Evelyn Torton. *Kafka and the Yiddish Theatre.* Madison: Wisconsin University Press, 1971.

Benjamin, Walter. "Franz Kafka: On the Tenth Anniversary of His Death" and "Some Reflections on Kafka," *Illuminations*, ed. Hannah Arendt, 111-46 New York: Schocken Books, 1969.

Booth, Wayne C. *The Rhetoric of Fiction.* Chicago: Chicago University Press, 1961.

Brod, Max. *Franz Kafka: A Biography.* Translated by G. Humphreys Roberts and Richard Winston. New York: Schocken Books, 1960.

Canetti, Elias. *Kafka's Other Trial: The Letters to Felice.* Translated by Christopher Middleton. New York: Schocken Books, 1974.

Cohn, Dorrit. "K. Enters *The Castle*: on the Change of Person in Kafka's Manuscript," *Euphorion*, 62 (1968): 28-45.

Collins, R.G. "Kafka's Special Methods of Thinking," *Mosaic*, 3 (1970): 43-57.

Corngold, Stanley. "Kafka's *Die Verwandlung*: Metamorphosis of the Metaphor," *Mosaic*, 3 (1970): 91-106.

Deleuze, Gilles, and Felix Guattari. *Kafka: Toward a Minor Literature.* Minneapolis: University of Minnesota Press, 1986.

Flores, Angel, ed. *The Kafka Problem.* New York: New Directions, 1946.

Flores, Angel, and Swander, eds. *Franz Kafka Today.* Madison: Wisconsin University Press, 1958.

Frye, Northrop. *Anatomy of Criticism.* Princeton: Princeton University Press, 1957.

Gray, Ronald. *Kafka's Castle.* Cambridge: Cambridge University Press, 1956.

————, ed. *Kafka: A Collection of Essays.* Englewood Cliffs, NJ: Prentice Hall, 1962.

Hirsch, E.D. Jr. *Validity in Interpretation.* New Haven: Yale University Press, 1967.

Janouch, Gustav. *Conversations with Kafka.* Translated by Goronwy Rees. London: Quartet Books, 1985.

Karst, Roman. "Franz Kafka: Word-Space Time," *Mosaic,* 3 (1970): 1-13.

Kermode, Frank. *The Sense of an Ending.* New York: Oxford University Press, 1967.

Koelb, Clayton. *Kafka's Rhetoric: The Passion of Reading.* Ithaca: Cornell University Press, 1989.

Leopold, Keith. "Breaks in Perspective in Franz Kafka's *Der Prozess,*" *GQ,* 36 (1963): 31-38.

Marson, Eric. *Kafka's "Trial:" The Case Against Joseph K.* St. Lucia, Australia: University of Queensland Press, 1975.

Murray, Jack. *Landscapes of Alienation: Ideological Deconstruction in Kafka, Celine, and Onetti.* Stanford: Stanford University Press, 1991.

Neider, Charles. *The Frozen Sea.* New York: Oxford University Press, 1948.

Politzer, Heinz. *Parable and Paradox.* Ithaca: Cornell University Press, 1962.

Robbins, Jill. *Prodigal Son/Elder Brother: Interpretation and Alterity in Augustine, Petrarch, Kafka, and Levinas.* Chicago: University of Chicago Press, 1991.

Robert, Marthe. *Franz Kafka's Loneliness.* Translated by Ralph Manheim. London: Faber and Faber, 1982.

Robertson, Ritchie. *Kafka: Judaism, Politics, and Literature.* Oxford: Clarendon Press, 1985.

Rolleston, James. *Kafka's Narrative Theater.* University Park: Pennsylvania State University Press, 1974.

———, ed. *Twentieth-Century Interpretations of "The Trial."* Englewood Cliffs, N.J.: Prentice-Hall, 1976.

Scholem, Gershom G. *Major Trends in Jewish Mysticism.* New York: Schocken Books, 1973.

Spann, Meno. *Franz Kafka.* World Author Series. Boston: G.K. Hall, 1976.

Spilka, Mark. *Dickens and Kafka: A Mutual Interpretation.* Bloomington: Indiana University Press, 1963.

Stern, J.P., ed. *The World of Franz Kafka.* London: Weidenfeld and Nicholson, 1980.

Sussman, Henry. *Franz Kafka: Geometrician of Metaphor.* Madison, Wis.: Coda Press, 1979.

Taubert, Herbert. *Franz Kafka: An Interpretation of His Works.* Translated by G. Humphreys Roberts and Roger Senhouse. New Haven: Yale University Press.

Udoff, Alan, ed. *Kafka and the Contemporary Critical Performance.* Bloomington: Indiana University Press, 1987.

West, Rebecca. *The Court and the Castle: Some Treatments of a Recurrent Theme.* New Haven: Yale University Press, 1957.

ACKNOWLEDGMENTS

"Preface," by Klaus Mann from *Amerika* by Franz Kafka, translated by Willa and Edwin Muir, copyright 1946 by Schocken Books. Copyright renewed 1974 by Schocken Books. Used by permission of Schocken Books, a division of Random House, Inc.

"*Amerika:* Its Meaning," by Lienhard Bergel. From *Franz Kafka Today*, eds.: Angel Flores and Homer Swander. © 1958 by The University of Wisconsin Press. Reprinted by permission.

"*Der Verschollene:* The Innocence of Karl Rossmann," by Heinz Politzer. From *Franz Kafka: Parable and Paradox*. Copyright © 1962, renewed 1990, revised and expanded 1976 by Cornell University. Used by permission of the publisher, Cornell University Press.

"Content Analysis of Kafka's Novels," by Calvin S. Hall and Richard E. Lind. From *Dreams, Life and Literature: A Study of Franz Kafka*. Copyright © 1970 by the University of North Carolina Press. Used by permission of the publisher.

"The dramatic in Kafka's work to 1914," by Evelyn Torton Beck. From *Kafka and the Yiddish Theater: Its impact on his work*. © 1971 by Evelyn Torton Beck. Reprinted by permission.

"*Amerika:* Literature as a Problem-solving Game," by Heinz Hillmann. From *The Kafka Debate: New Perspectives For Our Time*, ed. Angel Flores. © 1977 by Gordian Press. Reprinted by permission.

"The Urban World," by Ritchie Robertson. From *Kafka: Judaism, Politics, and Literature*. © 1985 by Clarendon Press. Reprinted by permission of Oxford University Press.

"Foreward," by E.L. Doctorow. From *Amerika*, by Franz Kafka, translated by Willa and Edwin Muir, copyright 1946 by Schocken Books. Copyright renewed 1974 by Schocken Books. Used by permission of Schocken Books, a division of Random House, Inc.

Themes and Ideas